5

# Christ & Israel

# CHRIST & ISRAEL

## An Interpretation of Romans 9-11

JOHANNES MUNCK

Foreword by KRISTER STENDAHL

FORTRESS PRESS          PHILADELPHIA

Translated from the Danish by Ingeborg Nixon

© 1967 by FORTRESS PRESS

*Library of Congress Catalog Card Number 67-17401*

*3946F67*     Printed in U.S.A.     *1-362*


This book has also been published in German under the title
*Christus und Israel—Eine Auslegung von Röm. 9-11*
(Copenhagen: Ejnar Munksgaard [*Acta Jutlandica*,
Publications of the University of Aarhus, Theology Series 7] 1956).

# FOREWORD

It is gratifying indeed that Johannes Munck's running commentary to Romans 9-11 becomes available to English readers. It was one of the preliminary studies in which Munck laid the groundwork for his magisterial interpretation of Paul, his role and self-understanding, *Paul and the Salvation of Mankind*. That volume, Munck's *magnum opus*, has for some reason come to play less of a role in the contemporary discussion of Pauline problems than it deserves. It has the character of a thesis with a distinctive thrust. Thus at points it pushes its case quite far; such a method of presentation irritates the pedantic reader, who finds it easy to feel superior because he can point to statements and interpretations that remain uncertain, doubtful, or perhaps just plain wrong. But no one can read Munck's study of Paul without feeling a genuine intellectual excitement. If I may speak in a more personal vein, it was the reading of this book more than twelve years ago which for the first time opened my eyes to Paul and his mission. It was the book that literally lifted hundreds of verses in the Pauline epistles out of a glorious haze of homiletical rhetoric and theological over-interpretation. It gave to the Pauline writings and to Paul the apostle a historical reality which—I hope—has remained with me ever since.

Munck's understanding of Paul has—in its simplest and most durable form—two foci. He sees Paul as conscious of a most elevated and crucial role in God's history with his people and with mankind. Paul is not just a missionary who out of a deep conversion experience became an unusually effective witness. He is *the* apostle to the Gentiles, handpicked by God for the pur-

pose, chosen and endowed like the great prophets of old. Perhaps we could say that this self-understanding reaches one of its
high points when in II Corinthians 3 the comparison given is not
one between Moses and Christ, but between Moses and *Paul*.

The other focus in Munck's understanding of Paul is best
understood if we reflect upon the chart which appears in this
book on page 123. Paul's special revelation, the mystery and the
gospel which he had received, was a reversal of the expected
timetable as to the salvation of Jews and Gentiles: rather than
letting the Yes of the Jews—which was not forthcoming at the
time—lead to the Yes of the Gentiles, Paul announced that the
very No of the Jews was God's strange way of bringing salvation to the Gentiles right then. And this in turn would, in God's
own time, lead to the Yes of the Jews.

It is around this question that Romans 9-11 circles, and thus
this running commentary to these central chapters constitutes a
most significant part of Munck's contribution. It is a careful and
lucid commentary, giving ample evidence of what was perhaps
Munck's greatest gift as a biblical scholar: the ability to read an
ancient text with fresh eyes. He was a born exegete in the precise sense of that word. It could also be argued that Munck's
image of Paul has its strongest support and its greatest ramifi-
cations in Romans, and more especially in these three chapters.

The reader of this study will slowly learn that Romans 9-11
is not what it has often been held to be in the history of Christian theology. It is not a tractate on the interesting theological
idea of predestination. It is rather Paul's attempt to give a rationale—a scriptural rationale—for God's plan as it was revealed
to Paul and as it unfolded itself in Paul's ministry. Nor is
Romans 9-11 an appendix to a famous tractate on justification
by faith. The statements about the famous righteousness of God
and the presentation in Romans 9-11 are both subservient to
Paul's primary concern of stating the principles behind his trav-
els and his mission. This statement is important, since he hopes

to visit the church in Rome (Romans 15), now that he plans to leave the East and come to the West.

There is a further reason why we should study these chapters in Romans, and we can do it well with Johannes Munck as a guide. Much has been done and said and written in recent years about the proper relationship between Jews and Christians. Few chapters from the New Testament are more directly addressed to this problem than the ones here under consideration. On the surface—and wrongly and satanically used—they can engender bitter feelings among Christians toward the Jews. But the thrust of Paul's argument is most certainly in the opposite direction. He is anxious to teach the Gentiles that *they* are the latecomers, the undeserving branches. "So do not become proud, but stand in awe" (Romans 11:20). In this connection it is important to note that to Paul the final Yes of the Jews is to be a miracle of God, reserved for God's own time. At no point does Paul urge the Gentiles to carry on a mission for the purpose of converting the Jews. The absence of such a note in Paul's letter is as striking as it is unexpected. I say "unexpected" because of the pattern of thought to which we have grown accustomed. But he who exposes himself, by means of the following study, to Paul's thinking in these three chapters of Romans will understand what I mean.

Johannes Munck was born in Copenhagen, Denmark, in 1904. He received his theological education at the University of Copenhagen, where he taught prior to becoming the first professor in the newly established Theological Faculty at the equally new University in Aarhus. There he remained until his death in 1965, becoming one of the architects of the university's academic program. He served as Rector, 1943-45.

His doctoral dissertation (1933) was a study of Clement of Alexandria. He often said that he had written it in a time when many scholars considered most New Testament problems solved once and for all—and thus he had been led to turn toward greener pastures. But he soon returned to his first love, the New Testament, and did so with an unusual feeling for the need to question the consensus—and the more established that consensus became, the more vigorously he questioned.

Johannes Munck's bibliography has been published in the international journal, *Studia Theologica*, 19 (1965), pp. 3-21.

KRISTER STENDAHL

*Harvard Divinity School*
*Cambridge, Massachusetts*
*March 1967*

# AUTHOR'S PREFACE

The material presented here is a study preliminary to my book, *Paulus und die Heilsgeschichte*, 1954 (English translation, *Paul and the Salvation of Mankind*, 1959, see p. xvii). Although this present study was begun in 1949 and completed in 1952, it was not prepared for publication until now because of a need to complete the larger work and because of a journey to Palestine and the Near East. Since the interpretation of Romans 9-11 contained in this preliminary study forms an important part of the basis for the conception of Paul and his apostolate advanced in *Paul and the Salvation of Mankind*, I feel it is only right now to publish this preliminary study as a survey of my understanding of Paul's ideas in these three chapters. In preparing it for publication I have done my best to take into consideration the literature published in the intervening years.

The aim of this interpretation is to take not a dogmatic, but an historical view, i.e., to maintain an awareness of the history contemporary to Paul. An attempt is made to understand Paul's problems and their solutions on the basis of life at that time, making wide use of late Jewish and New Testament parallels. On the latter point, the practice, common to the present day, of isolating Paul has not resulted in a definitive picture, and an attempt is therefore made to show that in this respect the apostle was also deeply rooted in the early Christian tradition.

JOHANNES MUNCK

*Aarhus, Denmark*
*May 1956*

# PREFATORY NOTE

The publication in English of my late husband's book *Christ and Israel* fulfills a wish that lay heavily upon his heart during the last year of his life. The German edition was no longer available, and my husband felt that the time had come for this book, which he regarded as basic to his Pauline research, to be brought to the wider audience of English-speaking readers. Tentative negotiations were begun with Fortress Press, and after Professor Munck's sudden death in February of 1965 I concluded those negotiations. From the very outset I was assured of the cooperation of my husband's esteemed translator, Dr. Ingeborg Nixon of Copenhagen. I want now to express my sincerest gratitude both to Dr. Nixon and to Dr. Niels Hyldahl of the University at Aarhus for their assistance in preparing the publication.

I wish also to express my heartfelt gratitude to my husband's American colleagues and to the students whose interest in *Paul and the Salvation of Mankind* encouraged him to make Christ and Israel available in English. Finally, to our friend Professor Krister Stendahl of Harvard University who has prepared the Foreword for this book, my deepest thanks.

ELISABETH MUNCK

*Aarhus*
*June 1967*

# TABLE OF CONTENTS

# LITERATURE AND ABBREVIATIONS

*N.B.* When in the present work authors are cited in *italics* and without bibliographical information, the reference is always to the appropiate work in the following selected bibliography.

## A. *Commentaries on Romans*

ALTHAUS, PAUL. *Der Brief an die Römer.* ("Neues Testament Deutsch.") 6th ed.; Göttingen: Vandenhoeck & Ruprecht, 1949.

BARDENHEWER, O. *Der Römerbrief des heiligen Paulus.* Freiburg: Herder, 1926.

BOYLAN, PATRICK. *St. Paul's Epistle to the Romans.* Dublin: M. H. Gill, 1934 (reprinted 1947).

DODD, C. H. *The Epistle to the Romans.* ("Moffatt New Testament Commentary.") New York: Harpers, 1932.

GAUGLER, ERNST. *Der Brief an die Römer.* ("Prophezei.") Zürich: Zwingli Verlag, 1945 and 1952.

HOLTZMANN, OSKAR (trans.). *Das Neue Testament,* Vol. II. Giessen: Töpelmann, 1926. Pp. 618-78.

JÜLICHER, ADOLF. *Der Brief an die Römer.* ("Die Schriften des Neuen Testaments," Vol. II.) 3rd ed.; Göttingen: Vandenhoeck & Ruprecht, 1917.

KUSS, OTTO. *Die Briefe an die Römer, Korinther und Galater.* ("Das Neue Testament," Vol. VI, Paulusbriefe I.) Regensburg: Pustet, 1940.

KÜHL, ERNST. *Der Brief des Paulus an die Römer.* Leipzig: Quelle & Meyer, 1913.

LAGRANGE, M.-J. *Épître aux Romains.* ("Études bibliques.") 3rd ed.; Paris: Gabalda, 1922.

LIETZMANN, HANS. *Einführung in die Textgeschichte der Paulusbriefe an die Römer.* ("Handbuch zum Neuen Testament," Vol. VIII.) 4th ed.; Tübingen: J. C. B. Mohr, 1933.

LYONNET, R. P. (trans.). *Les Épîtres de saint Paul aux Romains et aux Galates.* (La Sainte Bible, traduite a francais sous la direction de l'École biblique de Jerusalem.) Paris: Les Editions du Cerf, 1953.

MICHEL, OTTO. *Der Brief an die Römer.* ("Kritisch-exegetischer Kommentar über das Neue Testament," Vol. IV.) 10th ed.; Göttingen: Vandenhoeck & Ruprecht, 1955.

MOE, OLAF. *Apostelen Paulus's Brev till romarne.* 2nd ed.; Oslo, 1948.

NYGREN, ANDERS. *Commentary on Romans.* Translated by Carl C. Rasmussen. Philadelphia: Fortress, 1949.

PALLIS, A. *To the Romans.* Liverpool: Liverpool Booksellers' Co., 1920.

SANDAY, WILLIAM, AND HEADLAM, ARTHUR. *The Epistle to the Romans.* ("International Critical Commentary.") 5th ed.; Edinburgh: T. & T. Clark, 1920.

SCHLATTER, ADOLF. *Gottes Gerechtigkeit—Ein Kommentar zum Römerbrief.* Stuttgart: Calwer, 1935.

SICKENBERGER, J. *Die Briefe des heiligen Paulus an die Korinther und Römer.* ("Die Heilige Schrift des Neuen Testaments," Vol. VI.) 4th ed.; Bonn: Hanstein, 1932.

WEISS, B. *Der Brief an die Römer.* ("Kritisch-exegetischer Kommentar über das Neue Testament," Vol. IV.) 8th ed.; Göttingen: Vandenhoeck & Ruprecht, 1891.

ZAHN, THEODOR. *Der Brief des Paulus an die Römer.* ("Kommentar zum Neuen Testament," Vol. VI.) 1st and 2nd ed.; Leipzig: A. Deichert, 1910.

### B. Other Studies and References

BAUER, WALTER. *A Greek-English Lexicon of the New Testament and Other Early Christian Literature,* translated and adapted from the 4th German edition by William F. Arndt and F. Wilbur Gingrich. Chicago: University of Chicago Press, 1957. Abbreviated as *Bauer-Arndt-Gingrich.*

DIDERICHSEN, B. K. *Paulus Romansus—Et analytisk bidrag til Romerbrevets ældste historie.* Copenhagen, 1941.

GORE, CHARLES. "The Argument of Romans IX-XI," *Studia Biblica et Ecclesiastica,* III (1891), pp. 37-45.

HOPPE, THEODOR. "Die Idee der Heilsgeschichte bei Paulus mit besonderer Berücksichtigung des Römerbriefes," *Beiträge zur Förderung christliche Theologie,* XXX, 2 (1926).

KITTEL, GERHARD (ed.). *Theologisches Wörterbuch zum Neuen Testament.* Stuttgart: Kohlhammer, 1933 and continuing. Abbreviated as *Kittel (G).*

————. *Theological Dictionary of the New Testament.* Translated and edited by Geoffrey W. Bromiley. Grand Rapids: Eerdmans, 1964 and continuing. Abbreviated as *Kittel (E).*

LEKKERKERKER, A. F. N. *Römer 7 und Römer 9 bei Augustin.* Amsterdam, 1942.

MAIER, F. W. "Israel in der Heilsgeschichte / nach Röm. 9-11," *Biblische Zeitfragen* (Münster) XII, 11/12 (1929).

MUNCK, JOHANNES. *Paul and the Salvation of Mankind.* Translated by Frank Clarke. Richmond: John Knox, 1959. Abbreviated as PSM.

PETERSON, ERIK. "Die Kirche aus Juden und Heiden" (1933) *Theologische Traktate* (1951), pp. 239-92.

SCHMIDT, K. L. "Die Judenfrage im Lichte der Kapitel 9-11 des Römerbriefes," *Theologische Studien*, 13 (1943).

STRACK, HERMAN, AND BILLERBECK, PAUL. *Kommentar zum Neuen Testament aus Talmud und Midrasch*. 6 Vols. 2nd ed.; Munich: Beck, 1954-61. Abbreviated as *Billerbeck*.

VISCHER, WILHELM. "Das Geheimnis Israels. Eine Erklärung der Kapitel 9-11 des "Römerbriefs," *Judaica*, VI (1950), pp. 81-132.

WEBER, E. *Das Problem der Heilsgeschichte nach Röm. 9-11— Ein Beitrag zur historisch-theologischen Würdigung der paulinischen Theodizee*. 1911.

WEBER, VALENTIN. *Kritische Geschichte der Exegese des 9. Kapitels, resp. der Verse 14-23, des Römerbriefes bis auf Chrysostomus und Augustinus einschliessliche*. Würzburg, 1889.

# I. INTRODUCTORY REMARKS

# I. INTRODUCTORY REMARKS

## 1. The Letter to the Romans as a Manifesto of Faith

The various opinions about introductory matters connected with the letter to the Romans are of great importance for an understanding of the individual passages. It is therefore necessary to begin by mentioning what seem to me the most important of these questions. In a continuation of the efforts of the Tübingen School, scholars have regarded Romans as evidence of the contrast between Jewish and Gentile Christianity, either because the letter was written to a predominantly Jewish Christian church, or because the Roman church, while mainly Gentile, contained a large minority of Jewish Christians.

These views assume that the letter to the Romans, like the other Pauline letters, supplies evidence concerning the group of readers addressed. Thus it has been maintained that the subjects discussed in the letter prove that its readers must have been Jewish Christians, since those subjects are Jewish. They are questions concerning the validity of the law, the nature of salvation, the possibility of man's justification before God, and the election of Israel. Not only these questions, however, but also the manner and method in which they are handled, are designed to make an impression precisely upon Jews, since Old Testament teaching and Old Testament proofs mark Romans throughout.

There are great difficulties connected with this view. First

3

of all, Paul states, particularly in chapters 1 and 15, that he is addressing Gentile Christians in his letter. Secondly, in Galatians the same topics are enlarged upon to a group of Gentile Christian churches. The view in question derives from the assumption that the origin—religious, cultural, and national—of the readers can be deduced from the subjects dealt with in a letter. This assumption, however, has only a limited validity.

It overlooks the fact that Christianity, in its origin and early mission, including the mission to the Gentiles, was a new religion, decisively stamped by the Jewish, largely Palestinian environment out of which its missionaries generally came. At this early stage one cannot therefore speak of Gentile Christianity in the sense of a movement in the early church essentially different from Jewish Christianity, with a special preaching which was to form, for instance, the basis of Paul's mission and teaching. As subsequent missionary history shows, it is not until later (generations later, in most cases) that Christianity took root in the mission countries in such a way that there could be any question of an independent development either of its message or of ecclesiastical and social conditions in the field concerned.

If Hellenistic Judaism is put forward to explain an instantly arisen Gentile Christianity it must be objected that there are no grounds for assuming that the Judaism of the Greek diaspora differed essentially from Palestinian Judaism. It is as impossible to draw conclusions about Judaism in Egypt from Philo as it is to reconstruct Egyptian church history from Clement and Origen.

While the view discussed above seeks to explain the contents of the letter on the basis of a hypothetical group of readers who were mainly Jewish Christians, or who at any rate included a large minority of such within a predominantly Gentile Christian church, there are other scholars who seek to explain the letter on the basis of the author's intention, without reference to the recipients. They adduce as supporting evidence the fact that Romans differs from the other Pauline letters, and its intention must therefore be to set forth Christian doctrine and convince men of its truth. This view has played an important part in the interpretation of the letter, since Romans has to a large extent been treated as a theological tract, or even as a brief dogmatic treatise, so that attempts to understand the author's theological explanations in the context of a timeless, systematic line of thought have been given more attention than the discovery of its historical *Sitz im Leben*.

However, it is not necessary to confine ourselves to either of these two methods of procedure, each in its own way unsatisfactory. We do not need to explain the letter on the basis of circumstances in the church at Rome, which contrary to statements in the letter itself is said to include a Jewish Christian majority, or at any rate a large Jewish Christian minority. Nor do we need to sever the letter from every historical connection to the early Christian mission and regard it as a piece of timeless systematic theology.

T. W. Manson has sought a way to avoid these traditional attitudes to the problem.[1] Manson puts the question: Was Romans in its present form originally composed as *one* piece, expressly intended for the church in Rome, and sent to it in the form we now possess? In the oldest Pauline manuscript (p46) the doxology, which in the later text forms the conclusion, 16: 25-27, is placed at the end of chapter 15; from which fact it can be assumed that sometime previous to p46 there had been a text of the letter that did not include chapter 16. Such a text would corroborate the theory, put forward by David Schulz, that Romans 16 is a letter to the church at Ephesus. If Romans 1-15 is the letter Paul sent to Rome, then Marcion, who published his text of Paul in the West, would have removed only chapter 15 from his Roman original, since chapter 16 was not there to begin with.

The hypothesis that Romans 16 is a letter to the church at

---

[1] "St. Paul's Letter to the Romans—and Others," *Bulletin of the John Rylands Library*, 31 (1948), pp. 224-40.

Ephesus has powerful support in the light of its many greetings to friends and acquaintances, such as Paul would scarcely
have acquired in a church he had never visited. And those
friends whose names are already familiar to us have connec-
tions with Ephesus and Asia. The exhortation at 16:17-20
would also seem most natural addressed to a church which Paul
himself had founded and where he had stayed for several years.
The difficulty about this hypothesis, as Lietzmann in particular
has maintained, is that chapter 16, which consists almost entirely of greetings, could hardly be an independent letter.

But now that p46 has been published, light has also been
thrown upon this vexing question. It can now be assumed that
Paul, after writing and sending Romans 1-15 as a letter to
Rome, added chapter 16 to a copy of it and sent this to Ephesus.
This second letter still included the personal observations of
15:14-33—originally intended for the church in Rome—because these accounts of Paul's plans were also of interest to the
Christians in Ephesus. The additional chapter (16) contains
(1) a recommendation of Phoebe, who was presumably the
bearer of the letter to Ephesus, (2) the many greetings to Paul's
friends in Asia, and (3) the exhortation in vv. 17-20. These
additions are then combined with the first fifteen chapters
originally sent to Rome to form a complete "mailing" for
Ephesus. A transcript of this second letter came at an early date
to Egypt, where the Roman text (i.e., the first fifteen chapters)
was synthesized with the Ephesian text, which would have been
more familiar to the Egyptians. As p46 shows, the Roman text,
concluding with chapter 15, was enlarged by the addition of
chapter 16 from the Ephesian text.

Manson next assumes that Paul slanted the subject-matter
of Romans—not merely to Rome but to Ephesus as well, judging by the history of the text. Before the letter was written,
during the third journey, its questions had been a source of disagreement—a disagreement that opposed Judaism to Christianity and law to gospel. Moreover, these questions—discussed

also in Galatians, in Philippians 3, and in II Corinthians 3-6—
are now comprehensively and thoroughly treated in Romans
1-11. The substance of these chapters thus derives from the
controversy between Paul and his opponents. The same impression is given by the later sections of the letter, which also deal
with questions that have been treated earlier, viz., in correspondence with the church at Corinth.

These observations seem to show that Romans is essentially
a summary of the point of view that Paul had reached through
the long controversy during his third journey. When Paul had
composed this statement he decided to send a copy to his friends
in Ephesus, whom he did not intend to visit on his journey to
Jerusalem (Acts 20:3, 16). This copy was intended as information for the churches in Asia. At the same time he wanted
to send a copy to Rome, together with a description of his future
plans. Paul may have left a copy in Corinth, but it is possible
that he personally explained and discussed the contents of
Romans with the members of the church there.

Thus Paul has given the Corinthian church a complete oral
report, and the church in Syria and Palestine will soon hear it in
the same way. The church in Asia and the Roman church will
be informed in writing. Viewed in this light, Romans ceases
to be merely a letter in which Paul introduces himself to the
church in Rome. It rather becomes a manifesto proclaiming his
deepest convictions on vital matters and claiming the widest
publicity—to the attainment of which the apostle dedicates his
entire strength.

This investigation by T. W. Manson is of importance for the
future treatment of Romans. Instead of explaining the letter on
the basis of its readership—and an erroneous idea of the readership at that—or making the author's theological ideas the only
premise of the letter as a whole, a new and promising possibility has now been suggested: The letter may be understood
on the basis of the author's situation and background in the
Eastern world, a situation and background already familiar to

us from the letters he wrote on his third journey. Some interpreters, like the present author, may at some points differ from
Manson because of a varying interpretation of events on Paul's
third journey, but the advance made in interpreting Romans is
obvious.

## 2. Paul's Situation When Composing the Letter to the Romans

In this section Paul's situation at the time of the composition
of Romans will be treated only insofar as it is of importance
for understanding chapters 9-11. But the following observation
must be made: Paul's attitude toward both the Jewish and the
Gentile missions, as shown in Romans 9-11, makes it clear that
he is not merely absorbed in the details of missionary work;
rather, at this stage he views the whole mission situation from
a comprehensive knowledge and has an objective view of the
decisive factors: namely, Israel's unbelief and the Gentiles'
acceptance of the gospel. It is therefore correct to affirm that
the milieu of Romans is not just a confrontation between Judaism and Pauline Christianity,[2] but a three-way discussion in-
volving the Gentiles, Judaism, and Christianity. Romans thus
contains more than just an internal church debate, but in several passages involves a religious dialogue, principally between
Israel and the church.

As far as the external circumstances are concerned, Paul's
situation at the time of writing Romans is known from Acts.
He has come from Macedonia to Corinth, where he will spend
the three winter months before traveling to Jerusalem.[3] But
when he resumes his voyage he changes his route.

[2] Both the expansion and the importance of Judaism have been much exaggerated; see PSM, pp. 87-134, 279-281. Paul is also much more in agreement
with Palestinian Jewish Christianity than is commonly assumed; see *ibid.*,
*passim.*

[3] Acts 19:21; 20:2-3. The passages in question speak of Greece, not expressly of Corinth, but it is generally assumed that Corinth was the place,
since we know from II Cor. that Paul was on his way to this church when he
was in Macedonia.

A Jewish conspiracy against his life has caused him to abandon the plan of sailing directly to Syria. Instead, he goes by land through Macedonia, and then on by sea to Tyre (Acts 20:3, 6, 13-16; 21:1-3).

Thus, assuming the reliability of Acts, we can follow Paul almost step by step during these months. We are also, thanks to Romans (supplemented by Acts on certain points), quite well informed as to Paul's circumstances, thoughts, and plans. This winter residence in Corinth marks a turning point in Paul's work as an apostle to the Gentiles. He has just completed his work in the East and intends, after traveling to Jerusalem, to go via Rome to Spain, there to begin his work in the West (Romans 15:22-26). Simultaneously, this winter marks a climax. Paul has completed the great collection for the poor in the Jerusalem church and he is spending the winter in Greece together with representatives of the churches that took part in the collection.[4] The preparation of this collection during the third journey extended over several years and was hampered by difficulties in the very churches Paul had asked to participate. Judaism in the Galatian churches and the Corinthians' rebellion against Paul stopped the collection completely, at all events as far as the latter were concerned. Only at the last moment was Paul able to get it going again, and we must assume that conditions in the Galatian churches led to similar results.[5]

The completed collection is therefore, like the intended journey to Spain, a testimony to the happy resolution of conflicts he had experienced during the third journey. The strayed and rebellious churches had to be brought back to an untroubled

[4] II Cor. 8:16—9:5 shows that in the autumn before this winter Paul traveled through Macedonia to Achaia with various church representatives, some of whom he sent ahead to Corinth so that they could complete the collection satisfactorily before the apostle himself arrived with the Macedonian representatives in his party. According to Acts 20:4-5, Paul set out on the journey to Jerusalem with a large group of church representatives (for these delegates, see PSM, pp. 293-97).

[5] We do not know whether the collection could be resumed in the Galatian churches; see PSM, pp. 294-97.

communion with the apostle before he could resume the collection, and before he could leave these eastern regions. II Corinthians gives us the impression that the apostle was detained in the East because of his boundless patience and indulgence toward the church in Corinth.[6]

This collection is thus an expression of what had been achieved among the Gentiles in the East. The new churches demonstrated their confession of Christ and their brotherly communion with the church in Jerusalem by contributing to the support of its many poor.[7] Paul envisages two difficulties in connection with his approaching visit to Jerusalem: one is the church's reception of the gift, the other is the attitude of the unbelieving Jews toward the apostle during his visit (Romans 15:31).[8] Granted that the voluntary gift might be badly received in Jerusalem,[9] the Jews' opposition to the gospel and to

[6] We have no direct knowledge of the effect of II Cor. on the church. Greece, where Paul spent the winter (Acts 20:2), does not necessarily mean Corinth, and there are no delegates from Corinth among those mentioned by name in Acts 20:4. But L. J. Koch in *Fortolkning til Paulus' andet Brev til Korinthierne* (2nd ed.; Copenhagen, 1927), p. 55, is right in saying that II Cor. 10:15-16 shows that Paul wished to extend his ministry to the countries west of Achaia, but only on condition that the Corinthians' faith reached a greater maturity. Since Paul in Rom. 15:22, 24, 28 has decided to go to Rome and Spain, it must be assumed that there really had been significant progress in the spiritual life of Corinth. Indeed, Koch holds that this is more than a mere deduction, for in Rom. 15:23 Paul expressly states that "I no longer have any room for work in these regions" (which Koch takes to be Achaia, but in my opinion it is the whole of the East, including this province), and by this he can only mean that he has accomplished enough so that his work is no longer needed there, the church in Corinth now being on its feet.

[7] II Cor. 8-9 (especially 9:13).

[8] Concerning the Jews' persecution of Paul, see Excursus I, "Israel as Persecutor," below, pp. 49-55.

[9] This remark seems to rule out the possibility that the collection was an assessment exacted from the church in Jerusalem. For the arguments against this view, which was held by Karl Holl in "Der Kirchenbegriff des Paulus in seinem Verhältnis zu dem der Urgemeinde," *Gesammelte Aufsätze zur Kirchengeschichte* (Tübingen, 1928) II, 44-67, see PSM, pp. 287ff. In Acts 21:17-26—whether the text be interpreted traditionally or as suggested by me (PSM, pp. 238-42)—we see that there were difficulties in connection with the reception in Jerusalem. As regards Rom. 15:31, the two prayers may

Paul's mission to the Gentiles, which had now been his daily vocation for many years, would be even more likely to blaze up when he and the representatives of the Gentile Christian church arrived in Jerusalem with the collection.

These difficulties might seem to make the designated procedure quite impossible. The money could after all reach its destination without this crowd of church representatives and without the presence of Paul—the very two circumstances that would make the presentation of the collection an unconcealable public affair (Acts 21:22, "They will certainly hear that you have come"). The chosen procedure would surely elicit reactions from the population and the authorities at Jerusalem.

However, a more quiet presentation of the money would still attain some of the aims Paul had in mind for this collection. It is stated in II Corinthians 9:13-14, for instance, that the effect of the gift is to cause the Jewish Christians to thank God for the faith of the Gentile Christians, and pray for them and long for them; yet this could be achieved equally well without the presence of Paul, and also without any large deputation of donors. And the object of the journey—as provided by Manson's hypothesis—that Paul wished to talk with the church in Jerusalem about the result of his considerations at the end of the third journey's conflicts, have been achieved by a written report, such as that submitted to the churches in Rome and Ephesus.

The explanation for these two circumstances (that Paul goes to Jerusalem himself in spite of great personal danger[10] and that he is accompanied by a large party of representatives of the Gentile churches) is to be found in the view Paul expressed in Romans 11 concerning the connection between the mission to the Gentiles and the mission to the Jews. He desires to save the Jews by making them jealous of these Gentiles who are accepting the gospel in large numbers. And as he writes these

be connected, since being saved from the unbelievers is a prerequisite for handing over the gift without trouble.

[10] Rom. 15:31; Acts 20:3, 22-25; 21:11.

words he is waiting for the ship to take him and a delegation of Gentile believers to Jerusalem and to "the disobedient," as he calls them. Their traveling to Jerusalem with gifts has been prophesied: the Gentiles would thus arrive in the last days.[11]

This impending journey has set its mark on Romans in various ways. Not only does the letter contain (in chapter 11, as mentioned above) Paul's opinions about relations between the Gentile and Jewish missions but in the preceding chapter it gives us a picture of the Jewish mission at that period, a picture all the more valuable because we would otherwise have very little information on the subject. According to Romans 10:18, the messengers of Christ have gone out to the Jews all over the earth, and have everywhere met the same impenitence among the chosen people. Thus a few verses later (10:21) the prophet Isaiah is quoted with regard to Israel: "All day long I have held out my hands to a disobedient and contrary people."

Apart from these main features of the appraisal put forward by Paul at this juncture, a number of details in chapters 9-11 gain life and color when the object of Paul's journey is borne in mind. In 9:1-5 Paul says that he wishes he himself could be cut off from Christ for the sake of his brothers. As we shall see,[12] Paul is here speaking as a figure of redemptive history who, like Moses on Sinai, pleads for the people and declares himself ready to suffer vicariously the punishment they have earned.

In 9:26 Paul quotes Hosea 2:1 and adds an ἐκεῖ, which is a natural designation for Palestine, in order to imply that the Gentile nations will gather in Jerusalem and the Messianic kingdom will be established there (cf. 11:26). It is thus in Jerusalem, where the Gentiles were told, "You are not my people," that they will now be called "sons of the living God." Interpreted in this way, the words are of immediate importance to Paul who, with a delegation of Gentile believers, is at this

[11] Isa. 2:2-4 and Micah 4:1-4. Cf. PSM, pp. 303-05.
[12] Pp. 27-30 below.

very moment on his way to the holy city with gifts. His thought in this passage is that Israel will realize that God by his grace has accepted the Gentiles as his people, and that they will therefore be filled with the jealousy which, in Paul's eyes, opens the way to salvation determined by God.

Another Romans passage (10:10) has given trouble to exegetes: "For man believes with his heart and so is justified, and he confesses with his lips and so is saved." Why does Paul here speak of confession? There are many explanations,[13] but again the impending journey is probably the most natural. At this juncture the apostle had in mind the act of confessing before the authorities. He thought of the approaching journey to Jerusalem and of the approaching confession before his people— perhaps before the Sanhedrin—that this would involve.

Lastly, Romans 11:2 makes use of an Old Testament figure which both resembles Paul's situation at that moment and is yet essentially different. Elijah made intercession before God against Israel with the words, "Lord, they have killed thy prophets, they have demolished thy altars, and I alone am left, and they seek my life" (11:3, cf. I Kings 19:10). Bloody persecutions, instigated by the Jews, had afflicted the church, and the closing words of the quotation (that the Jews sought his life) were only too true in Paul's case. Like the prophet, he confronts a majority of the people, alone and in danger of death. And just as Elijah returned from his stay among the Gentiles in order to settle matters between Baal and Yahweh through the test of power on Mount Carmel, so Paul is now on his way from the Gentiles so that stubborn Israel may be shown the obedience of faith as it is to be found among the Gentile believers. But an important thing to see is that Paul has not, like Elijah, made intercession before God against Israel; rather, his desire and prayer before God is the salvation of the Jews (9:1-5; 10:1).

[13] See pp. 88-89 below.

### 3. Israel's Unbelief: a Primitive Christian Problem

One result of that isolation of Paul from Jewish Christianity which scholarship has commonly asserted since the time of the Tübingen School is that Paul's problems and reflections in Romans 9-11 are generally treated out of context with the rest of the New Testament. There has been a tendency to overlook these chapters, or at any event Paul's optimistic view of Israel's future. In general, study of these chapters, and of parallel and similar passages elsewhere in the New Testament, has suffered from a failure to compare the texts and thus allow them to shed light on each other.

It is not my intention to do this in any detail here. That would require a comprehensive account, and I hope to consider on another occasion the wider context to which this question belongs. Here I shall merely attempt to show that Paul's problem, and several of the individual questions involved, are treated in the Gospels; apart from this, the reader is referred to the passages, especially from the Gospels and Acts, cited *passim* in the exposition below.

As regards the question in 9:6, whether God's promise has lapsed, a basic problem in primitive Christianity was this question of whether the Old Testament, regarded as Holy Writ by Jews and Christians alike, can be a true revelation from God when Israel after the flesh has not accepted the promised Messiah and his salvation, and the promises uttered by God concerning the chosen people have thus not been fulfilled. Like Paul, primitive Christianity solved the problem through its interpretation of the Old Testament. This interpretation was based upon God's revelation in Christ and viewed everything in that light. Christ's life and ministry, his death and resurrection, the church as the new people of God, and its life in this world, are all foretold in the Old Testament. The time of Jesus and the apostles is the time of the fulfillment of all God's promises. The problem is whether these promises also apply to Israel after the flesh—for in the middle of the time of fulfillment this people is marked by obduracy and unbelief. Both in primitive Christianity and in Paul we find an interpretation of the Old Testament that allows Israel to retain a special position in the time of the new covenant. And yet Paul, like the Evangelists, is convinced of God's sovereign election, and agrees with the words of John the Baptist that God is able from these stones to raise up children to Abraham (Matthew 3:9; Luke 3:8).

The next question (9:14-21) is whether God's sovereign election of one covenant people but not of the other can be justified. This contradiction in the picture of God is familiar to us from the Gospels. The "father" or "king" figure in the parables of Jesus in many cases shows God to differ from the Jewish conception of him. He acts in surprising ways, and from the Jewish point of view these ways are unjust. Thus we have the conduct of the father in the parable of the prodigal son (Luke 15:11-32), the odd king in the parable of the two debtors (Matthew 18:23-35), and the householder in the parable of the wicked husbandmen (Matthew 21:33-41). But above all there is the parable of the laborers in the vineyard (Matthew 20:1-16). In this story the strangeness of the householder's action is obvious and gives rise to "grumbling" on the part of those laborers who are to have the same pay as the others, even though they have worked all day long and the others started later. The householder's retort is significant (vv. 13-15), "Friend, I am doing you no wrong; did you not agree with me for a denarius? Take what belongs to you, and go; I choose to give to this last as I give to you. Am I not allowed to do what I choose with what belongs to me? Or do you begrudge my generosity?" It is clear that with this conclusion the parable raises a fundamental question concerning God's sovereignty over man. Man—that is, the Jew—knows what is just; but this strange householder, the Father of our Lord Jesus Christ, dismisses the human concept of justice. The words,

"Am I not allowed to do what I choose with what belongs to me?" might have been written in Romans 9.

It may be added that there is in the Palestinian Talmud a story, which can be regarded as a Jewish answer to Jesus' parable.[14] Here it is a king who hires many laborers. There is one particularly diligent laborer whom the king takes with him, away from the task. And when in the evening all the laborers are given the same wages, the other laborers grumble, as in Jesus' parable, and say, "We have worked the whole day, and this man has worked only two hours, and he has given full wages like us!" But the king gives an answer that shows that the apparent injustice is in fact true justice, "This man has worked more in two hours than you have done throughout the whole day."

The use of the image of the potter for God and his all-powerful dispositions (Roman 9:20 ff.) brings to mind the words of John the Baptist, "And do not presume to say to yourselves, 'We have Abraham as our father'; for I tell you, God is able from these stones to raise up children to Abraham" (Matthew 3:9).

The idea of God's longsuffering (9:22) is to be found in the parable of the fig tree (Luke 13:6-9) where the dresser of the vineyard is granted a year's respite before the tree is cut down. This story is set in a speech of which the refrain is: unless you repent you will all likewise perish.[15]

As mentioned below,[16] a number of scholars believe that the Old Testament concept of the remnant can be found in the Gospels. It is an obvious idea, but as yet no decisive proof for this point of view has been given.

The account of the Jews' pursuit of the law, in which they stumbled against Christ (Romans 9:30—10:4), is made visible

[14] Berakhoth 2, 5c, 15; *Billerbeck* IV, 1, 492-93.

[15] Coming from Romans, with its οὐ πάντες (9:6), one notices in Luke 13:3, 5 the phrase, "You will *all* likewise perish."

[16] Excursus II, pp. 111-12.

in the Gospels by their frequent descriptions of clashes between the Jews and Jesus concerning the law and the traditions of their fathers. In Matthew 21:42 Christ is likewise the stumblingstone,[17] while verse 44 of that chapter gives a more hopeless picture of the fate of the stumblers than does Paul.

Romans 10 deals with the period after the death and resurrection of Jesus when the apostles go out into the world with the gospel. At a later point in our exposition[18] attention will be drawn to the fact that Paul, like the speakers in the sermons in Acts, assumes that the death of Jesus, brought about by the Jews in their ignorance (cf. Romans 10:3), does not involve the lasting exclusion of the Jews from salvation; rather—by raising Jesus from the dead—God has given the Jews the possibility of receiving salvation.

There may be disagreement as to details between Paul and our other primitive Christian sources—for instance, Romans 10:18 presumes that the apostles to the Jews have reached Israel in all the world, while Matthew 10:23 states that the disciples who have been sent out will not come to the end of the cities of Israel before the coming of the Son of Man—but Israel's unbelief and obduracy are described in the Gospels, and much more drastically than by Paul in Romans 9-11. We hear of the lack of obedience of the Jews, and the hardening of their hearts,[19] of their not hearing and their not understanding.[20] We learn that the Gentiles accept the gospel while the Jews, "the children of the kingdom," are cast out.[21] God's

[17] From Psalm 118:22-23, not Isaiah 28:16 or 8:14. See p. 80 below.

[18] Pp. 79-84 below.

[19] Cf. for instance the use of the expression "this generation" in Matt. 11:16 f.; Mark 8:12; Matt. 17:17, Mark 9:19, Luke 9:41; Matt. 23:36, Luke 11:50-51; Mark 8:38; Luke 17:25. Also Acts 2:40; Phil. 2:15; Heb. 3:10. Hardening of hearts is mentioned in Mark 3:5 (of the disciples, Mark 6:52; 8:17); John 12:40.

[20] The senses of the Jews are dulled so that they cannot see and hear, and they cannot grasp the new message. See below pp. 99-102.

[21] E.g., Matt. 8:11-12, Luke 13:28-29. See also the story of the Canaanite woman, especially in Matthew's version, 15:21-28 (cf. PSM, pp. 260-64).

words in Isaiah 65:2—"All day long I have held out my hands to a disobedient and contrary people"—have close parallels in sayings of Jesus.[22]

Considering that chapter 11 deals with the problems of the Gentile Christians in relation to Israel's present status, i.e., since the coming of Christ, one might expect it to lack any parallels in the Gospels. This, however, is not the case. The problem of the remnant (Romans 11:1 ff.) has been noted above, and the effect of the hardening of the heart on the eyes and ears (Romans 11:7 f.) has been mentioned also.[23] Psalm 69, on the other hand, which is quoted by Paul in 11:9-10, has not yet been mentioned. This is one of the Psalms which the earliest church interpreted as referring to the passion of Christ. It is interesting that Paul does not draw from the Psalm what would seem to be an obvious conclusion: that because the Jews have crucified the Lord Jesus (Psalm 69:21) the wrath of God shall fall upon Israel forever (69:22 ff.). Paul differs from what was probably the common interpretation of this psalm among early Christians, because he knows that God has not cast away his people forever.[24]

The heavy stress laid on Israel's great importance to the Gentiles (11:11 ff.) is a link with Jewish thought,[25] and is reminiscent of the view of missionary work held by Jewish Christianity in Jerusalem: "To the Jew first, and also to the Greek," quoted by Paul in Romans 1:16; 2:9-10. According to Acts 15 this Jerusalem view is expressed by James at the meeting in Jerusalem, where he quotes Amos 9:11 ff. God will first build again the fallen tabernacle of David in order that the rest of mankind may seek the Lord. Israel, in other words, must

22 E.g., Matt. 23:37, Luke 13:34.

23 See also pp. 99-102 below.

24 See pp. 114-16 below.

25 Cf., for instance, Paul Volz, *Die Eschatologie der jüdischen Gemeinde im neutestamentliche Zeitalter* (2nd ed.; Tübingen: J. C. B. Mohr, 1934) pp. 356-59.

accept Christ first, so that through them salvation may come to the Gentiles.

The story of the olive tree in Romans 11:17 ff., which makes clear the unity between the elect of the old and new covenants, is clearly different from both Jesus' parable (Luke 13:6-9) of the fig tree (that is, Israel) and his symbolic treatment of the fig tree (also Israel) in Matthew 21:18-22.

The earliest disciples assumed that the gospel was to be preached to Israel, and that Israel's acceptance of Jesus as the Messiah would also determine the salvation of the Gentiles. Paul has a different view: on account of Israel's unbelief he gives prominence to the mission to the Gentiles as an expression of God's will that salvation should come first to the Gentiles and then to Israel. In the Gospels it is clearly stated that the gospel is to be preached to Israel—if not exclusively, then at least first.[26] In addition we have some comprehensive and horrifying evidence of the people's unbelief and of the hardening of their hearts.

The Gospels, in the form in which we possess them, present a composite picture that may be described as follows: In accordance with its privileged position Israel was offered the gospel, but it rejected God's salvation and crucified the Messiah sent by him, and now awaits God's judgment; simultaneously the risen Christ sends forth his twelve disciples, whose ministry was originally intended for the twelve tribes, to all the Gentiles throughout the earth—in order to bring them the salvation already offered to Israel but refused by them.

This inclination toward the Gentile mission and demonstration of Israel's obduracy as expressed in the editing of the Gospels cannot be a reflection of Jewish Christianity in Jerusalem, judging from what we know of it in Paul's epistles and in Acts. Either it belongs to a later stage in the development of Jewish Christianity, or else it is an interpretation of the tradition taken over from Jewish Christianity by Gentile Christians.

26 PSM, pp. 255-64.

In any event, the New Testament gives us a worked-over account of Jesus' sayings concerning the Jews and the Gentiles, which was necessitated by Israel's obduracy—the greatest problem faced by primitive Christianity. I have tried to show elsewhere what was done with the pericope of the Canaanite woman, and how the story of Cornelius in Acts 10 was heavily adapted even before Luke gave it its final interpretation in his editing of Acts.[27]

The Gospels, besides containing the idea of preaching the gospel to Israel alone—or to Israel first—also give extensive evidence of the obduracy of the chosen people. Thus they echo two of the main themes of Romans 9-11. There can be no doubt that the early church's discussion of Israel's fate had an influence on the transmission of Jesus' words and deeds and on the final shaping of the tradition as found in our four Gospels. We must therefore put the question whether the Gospels also contain the third main theme of Romans 9-11, viz., that Israel in spite of their unbelief will yet be saved.

As mentioned above, the structure of the Gospels seems to indicate otherwise. There are, nevertheless, two brief texts that suggest that Paul was not alone in the hope he expressed in Romans 11, making it an open question whether Paul has here reflected a common view, which apart from such instances has not been included in the Gospel tradition, or whether, as Paul's personal view, it has left traces in the Gospels. Possibly what we have in the Gospels may even be the mere relic of an earlier and more definite expectation within the tradition.

The first of the two texts is to be found in Matthew 23:39 (Luke 13:35), "For I tell you, you will not see me again, until you say, 'Blessed be he who comes in the name of the Lord.'" Like so many other Gospel texts, this and its context (23:37-39) have been interpreted in widely different ways. It is, however, quite generally interpreted as a reference to the coming of Jesus in glory, the assumption being that Israel is to be converted before the second coming.[28]

The second text to which reference may be made is Luke 21:24, "They will fall by the edge of the sword, and be led captive among all nations; and Jerusalem will be trodden down by the Gentiles, until the times of the Gentiles are fulfilled." Many commentators interpret the last sentence as referring to the Gentile rule over Jerusalem, while others hold that it is also a reference to the time of the conversion of the Gentiles.[29] If in the Gospels the context is of decisive importance for the understanding of the single verse, the first interpretation is to be preferred. But if we abandon so dubious a principle where a composite text like Luke 21:5 ff. is concerned, it is possible

[28] Thus Bernhard Weiss, *Das Matthäus Evangelium* ("Kritisch-exegetischer Kommentar, I," 8th ed.; Göttingen: Vandenhoeck & Ruprecht, 1890); Johannes Weiss, *Das Matthäus Evangelium* ("Die Schriften des Neuen Testaments, I," 3rd ed.; Göttingen: Vandenhoeck & Ruprecht, 1917); J. Schniewind, *Das Evangelium nach Matthäus* ("Das Neues Testament Deutsch," Göttingen: Vandenhoeck & Ruprecht, 1937); Alfred Plummer, *An Exegetical Commentary on the Gospel According to S. Matthew* (London and New York, 1909); *L'Évangile selon Saint Matthieu*, translated by P. Benoit ("La Sainte Bible," 2nd ed.; Paris: L'École Biblique de Jérusalem, 1953). B. Weiss alone assumes that the promise of the second coming presupposes the conversion of Israel and that this condition makes the second coming a problematical matter rather than a prophecy. J. Weiss, Schniewind, and Benoit refer to Rom. 11:25 f.

[29] The first interpretation is to be found in the following works: Bernhard Weiss, *Die Evangelien des Markus und Lukas* ("Kritisch-exegetischer Kommentar," I, 2nd ed.; Göttingen: Vandenhoeck & Ruprecht, 1892); Alexandros Pallis, *Notes on Saint Luke and the Acts* (London: Humphrey Milford, 1928); William Manson, *The Gospel of Luke* ("Moffatt New Testament Commentaries," New York: Harpers, 1930); Lyder Brun, *Lukas-Evangeliet*, (Oslo, 1933); Friedrich Hauck, *Das Evangelium des Lukas* ("Theologische Handkommentar zum Neuen Testament," III, Leipzig: A. Deichert, 1934) p. 255; Josef Schmid, *Das Evangelium nach Lukas* ("Regensburger Neue Testament," III, 3rd ed.; Regensburg, 1955). A reference to the times of the Gentile conversion is to be found in the following: Erich Klostermann, *Das Lukas-Evangelium* ("Handbuch zum Neuen Testament," 2nd ed.; Tübingen: J. C. B. Mohr, 1929); H. J. Holtzmann, *Die Synoptiker* ("Hand-commentar zum Neuen Testament," I, 1, 3rd ed.; Freiburg, 1889-91); *L'Évangile selon Saint Luc* ("La Sainte Bible," Paris: L'École Biblique de Jérusalem, 1956); and very cautiously in M.-J. Lagrange, *Évangile selon Saint Matthieu* ("Études Bibliques," 7th ed.; Paris, 1948).

that the second interpretation should be chosen.[30] We should then have the same idea as in Romans 11, namely, that the Gentiles are to receive the gospel before Israel. In Luke, however, the political and religious history of Israel go together in a way not found in Paul.

These two texts—particularly the second—are doubtful proof that the view expressed in the Gospels is the same as that of Romans 11. But there is one conclusion we can draw in our present discussion, namely, that it must have been difficult for the Gospels to preserve, without ambiguity, any optimistic pronouncements as to the final salvation of hardened Israel. It is not surprising, then, that there should be some doubt as to the interpretation of the two above texts.

[30] Ezekiel 30:3-4 does not seem to support an interpretation of "the times of the Gentiles" as referring to the period when the Gentiles have Jerusalem in their power.

# II. EXEGESIS OF ROMANS 9-11

# Summary Outline of Romans 9-11

| | |
|---|---|
| 9:1-5 | Lament over Israel |
| 9:6-13 | The Jews cannot claim salvation as a right* |
| 9:14-21 | For God alone determines salvation and damnation* |
| 9:22-29 | But God has in fact acknowledged a remnant of Israel and the Gentiles* |
| 9:30—10:4 | The Gentiles received salvation, but not the Jews since they would not follow God's way of salvation in Christ* |
| 10:5-13 | God requires only faith in the heart and its confession on the lips* |
| 10:14-21 | God has caused the gospel to be preached by apostles to the Jews throughout the earth, but they have not accepted it* |
| 11:1-10 | Does this mean that Israel has been rejected? No, there is a chosen remnant left* |
| 11:11-27 | Was it the will of God that the Jews should fall? No, but the salvation of the Gentiles was the first result of the Jews' unbelief, and it is God's plan that the fullness of the Gentiles shall in time call forth the salvation of all Israel* |
| 11:28-32 | For God's way of salvation is disobedience and then mercy, and thus God saves all men |
| 11:33-36 | Final doxology |

* with proof from the Scriptures

# II. EXEGESIS OF ROMANS 9-11

### 9:1-5: Lament over Israel[1]

There is no direct connection with the preceding passage: no transitional formula has been provided, and there is no change in tone. After the joyful conclusion of chapter 8, Paul plunges at once into an expression of deep sorrow. This is hardly accidental. In the midst of his joy that nothing can separate "us" from God's love in Christ, Paul breaks off in order to express his sorrow that there is one exception to the company of those who have been saved, namely the chosen people Israel. He thereupon embarks on a theme indicated at the beginning of the letter: the Jew first, and then the Greek (1:16; 2:9-10; cf. 3:9; 9:24; 10:12). When we arrive at the doxology that ends chapter 11 (vv. 33-36) we know that Israel is not an exception. The love of God is as merciful toward the Jews as it is toward the Gentiles.

Paul expresses deep sorrow at the fate of his people, and says that he could wish himself cut off from Christ for the sake of his kinsmen by race.[2] From this one may conclude that

---

[1] *Schlatter* and *Sanday and Headlam* rightly compare Paul's lament here with the laments in IV Esdras 8:15; 10:6-8, 21-22 and in the Syriac Apocalypse of Baruch 35:1-5. The patristic exegesis of Rom. 9 is treated by *V. Weber* and *Lekkerkerker* as well as by K. H. Schelkle, "Erwählung und Freiheit im Römerbrief nach der Auslegung der Väter," *Theologische Quartalschrift*, 131 (1951), pp. 20-25.

[2] For ηὐχόμην and the line of thought in v. 3, see O. Michel, "Opferbereitschaft für Israel" in W. Schmauch, ed., *In Memoriam Ernst Lohmeyer* (Stuttgart, 1951) pp. 94-100.

it is the fate of those kinsmen to be outcasts from Christ.[3] But
we still have to be informed why and how this has happened.
This abrupt change of subject to the fate of the Jewish people,
though dimly defined, has a very practical reason. For it is only
gradually that Paul manages to explain to his readers, in light
of their many possible misunderstandings of the situation, what
the actual fate of his people is to be. A definition at the beginning of the passage would therefore be inadequate or confusing.
Nor is Paul free to follow his own line of thought: behind
him are innumerable discussions which are now to be crys-
tallized. Paul is not confronting particular flesh-and-blood
opponents—least of all in the church at Rome, which was un-
familiar to him—but he is thinking of all his opponents,
great and small, within and without the church, as he attempts
to reach definitive formulas for addressing Jews and Christians.

On the basis of Billerbeck's findings, *Lietzmann* has suggested that Paul's expression—that he could wish to be cut off
from Christ for the sake of his fellow countrymen—may be a
rabbinical expression of deep love, meaning that the speaker
will take upon himself another's retribution for the life to come.
To this suggestion of Lietzmann's it must be objected that the
parallels cited by *Billerbeck*, one or more of which state that
they will atone for a single dead person, are not actual parallels,[4]
quite apart from the fact that in some of these examples the
expression does seem to be a purely conventional phrase.[5] One

[3] Cf. Rom. 9:27-29; 10:3, 16; 11:1 ff., 8, 11, 25. It is remarkable that
Pauline research has never taken Paul seriously. For instance, the Pauline
churches have always been held to be mixed churches, with Jews sometimes
and Gentiles sometimes in the majority. But scholars have been skeptical of
Paul's statement, e.g., here in Rom. 9-11, that the Jews are without faith
while the Gentiles accept the gospel. New Testament scholars would achieve
clearer results if they would believe Paul and reckon with Gentile Christian
churches (see PSM, pp. 200-08).

[4] *Billerbeck*, III, 261. Lyder Brun in *Segen und Fluch im Urchristentum*,
(Oslo, 1932) pp. 127-28 rejects this analogy because Paul uses the sharp
expression ἀνάθεμα, and then adds ἀπὸ τοῦ χριστοῦ. Brun finds an explanation
for ἀνάθεμα in the fact that Paul was himself cursed by the Jews.

cannot compare the expression by an individual that he will atone for another with the expression by an individual that he will atone for all Israel. And even in N<sup>e</sup>g 2:1 the wish of R. Jischmael to atone for Israel is a conventional remark.[6] How could a single person possibly atone for the people?

On the other hand there are, according to *Billerbeck*,[7] some parallels to what Paul says in Romans 9:3, since here we have a reference to the fact that Jonah himself had said: "Take me up and cast me forth into the sea." Moses, David, Ezekiel, and Job all suffered vicariously for the people. Those concerned here are figures of redemptive history under the old covenant.

*Billerbeck* also quotes examples of vicarious suffering from IV Maccabees 1:11; 6:28 f.; 17:20 ff. But of the material here quoted by Billerbeck the most important is R. Hoshaiah's statement, according to which God said: "I take from the midst of them *one* righteous and pledge him for them and create for them [through this man] atonement for all their sins, etc."[8]

In my opinion there can be no doubt that in Romans 9:1 f. Paul is speaking of himself as a figure in New Testament *Heilsgeschichte*, and that despite a lack of linguistic parallels there is a parallel between Moses and Paul. In Exodus 32:31-32 it is stated, "So Moses returned to the Lord and said, 'Alas, this people have sinned a great sin; they have made for themselves gods of gold. But now, if thou wilt forgive their sin—and if not, blot me, I pray thee, out of thy book which thou hast written.' " The resemblance between this passage and the pas-

---

[5] Thus in Sanhedrin 2.1; Quidduschin 31 b Bar; Sukkah 20a (cf. *Billerbeck*, III, 261; also II, 164, 275, 279-80).

[6] In *The Babylonian Talmud, Seder Tohoroth II*, edited by Isidore Epstein and translated by Israel W. Slotki (London: Soncino Press, 1948) p. 238, note 7; Nega'im 2:1 is explained as follows: the expression "May I be an atonement for them" is "an expression of love and homage. 'May I be the victim making atonement for any punishment that may have to come upon them.' " (Cf. *Billerbeck*, III, 261, II, 280 and S Nu 35, 34 §161 [62 b].)

[7] II, 280-81 (note i).

[8] Ex R 35 (95 a). Cf. *Billerbeck*, II, 279-80.

sage in Romans lies in the solemnity with which the *heils-geschichtliche* figure offers himself as a substitute.

In both situations it is not a question of atoning for the ordinary everyday sins of the people. The wish of both Moses and Paul to suffer for their people arises from a situation where those people have sinned unforgivably. In Exodus, after the solemn establishment of the covenant on Sinai, the people do not have the patience to wait until Moses comes back from the mountain with the tables of the law; they make a bull calf and offer sacrifice to it. Similarly, the coming of the Messiah at the establishment of the new covenant is the moment when Israel again displays its disobedience in a time of grace. What punishment did Israel deserve for this disobedience if not destruction? But on both occasions a *heilsgeschichtliche* figure pleads for the people and offers to suffer the deserved punishment vicariously.

In the light of this, it is evident that the private cases, where one individual offers to atone for another, cannot—as Lietzmann assumes—be considered parallels to Romans 9:3. In the two examples from *Heilsgeschichte* to which attention has been drawn, it is the people of Israel who have committed an unforgivable sin, and Moses and Paul offer to make expiation. The individual cases, insofar as they have not become pure convention, belong to the Jewish penitential system, where a certain degree of penance can be served out. In the case of Moses and Paul it is a matter of salvation and damnation.

All the benefits mentioned in 9:4-5 as evidence of God's graciousness toward Israel belong to the early times of Israel's history,[9] just as Paul elsewhere prefers to make use of examples

---

[9] Lucien Cerfaux differs in "Le privilège d'Israel selon s. Paul," *Ephemerides Theolocicae Lovanienses*, 17 (1940), p. 7 (cf. p. 6, note 3); this is reprinted in *Recueil Lucien Cerfaux*, Vol. II (Gembloux, 1954) p. 341 (cf. p. 340, note 1): "One can only conclude that the Pauline enumeration in Rom. 9:4 is at least partly oriented toward the main thesis of his epistle. In other words, Paul is emphasizing patriarchs, covenant, and promises at

from Israel's history.[10] These early benefits given to Israel are: the name of Israelite,[11] the election as sons,[12] the *shekinah*,[13] the covenants[14] (from Abraham to Moses), the giving of the

the expense of the law. Adoption and glory thus assume a major role in his theology, and the privileges of Judaism find their full flowering within the Christian church."

[10] Though Paul does not, like the Palestinian rabbis, use the Pentateuch first and foremost (Joseph Bonsirven, *Exégèse rabbinique et exégèse paulinienne* ["Bibliothèque de théeologie historique"], Paris, 1939, p. 291), his treatment of Israel's history within the limited material of his letters is primarily directed toward the early period, from the patriarchs to Moses and the wilderness generation. The mention of Elijah in Rom. 11:2 f., for instance, is an exception.

[11] The name "Israelite" is applied by Paul to himself (Rom. 11:1) and to the bad apostles in Corinth (II Cor. 11:22). It is used in the New Testament only of Jews.

[12] υἱοθεσία is here used of Israel; otherwise the term is always used in the New Testament of Christians (Rom. 8:15, 23; Gal. 4:5; Eph. 1:5). The word does not occur in the LXX.

[13] Cf. the cloud in I Cor. 10:2. In the New Testament II Cor. 3:7 and Heb. 3:3 seem to attribute a δόξα to something in the Old Testament, but in both cases this is done in order to show how much less glorious the old covenant was in comparison with the new.

[14] L. Cerfaux, *op. cit.*, p. 13 (*Recueil Lucien Cerfaux*, II, 348) prefers the well-attested reading ἡ διαθήκη, and supplies extensive material to account for his preference. But when the covenants established in Genesis (cf. Lev. 26:42) are taken into account, the plural here makes excellent sense, since what immediately follows concerns the individual patriarchs with whom God made a covenant (9:6-13). Moreover, it is not merely διαθῆκαι, but also ἐπαγγελίαι, the other plural in a list of singular words, that is altered to the singular form in the transmitted text. In the New Testament there are only two covenants, the new and the old (Heb. 9:15: the first [πρώτη]), apart from Eph. 2:12, ξένοι τῶν διαθηκῶν τῆς ἐπαγγελίας. In the LXX the singular is likewise the normal form; there seems to be one covenant, any new establishment being merely a renewal of the already existing covenant. The only way of attaining a kind of plural is by adding together several covenant establishments, thus Lev. 26:42, μνησθήσομαι τῆς διαθήκης Ιακωβ καὶ τῆς διαθήκης Ισαακ καὶ τῆς διαθήκης Αβρααμ κτλ. Such an expression as τῆς διαθήκης τῆς προτέρας (Lev. 26:45) is probably an incorrect translation of ברית ראשנים. Not until late Jewish writings do we find as a result of reflection διαθήκη, in the plural (thus the Wisd. of Sol. 18:22; Sirach 44:12, 18; 45:17; II Macc. 8:15). Ezek. 16:29 τὰς διαθήκας (A: τὴν διαθήκην) does not reflect the Hebrew text, which is better given by the readings τὰς πορνείας or τὴν πορνείαν (cf. *Ezekiel*, ed. J. Ziegler in *Septuaginta*, XVI, 1 [Göttingen, 1952] p. 151); thus the corresponding Hebrew word in Ezek. 16:15, 22, 25, 33, 34, 36 is rendered by πορνεία in the singular. Rabbinical literature is also familiar with "covenants" in the plural (cf. *Billerbeck*, III, 262).

law at Sinai,[15] worship in the tabernacle during the wanderings in the wilderness, the promises,[16] and the patriarchs.[17]

Paul then leaps from early times to the last days—the days of fulfillment, when all promises shall be fulfilled to Israel through the Messiah, Christ,[18] who according to the flesh was of Israel, but who is at the same time God over all (for the wording, cf. Ephesians 4:6). What is noteworthy in 9:5—that Christ is termed $\theta\epsilon\acute{o}\varsigma$—has led to an interpretation of the text as a doxology to the Father, something which linguistically is not natural.[19] Although the designation $\theta\epsilon\acute{o}\varsigma$ is not used elsewhere by Paul of Christ, and one would therefore have expected another term for his heavenly origin in contradistinction to his origin in Israel $\kappa\alpha\tau\grave{\alpha}$ $\sigma\acute{\alpha}\rho\kappa\alpha$, it cannot, in my opinion, be denied that Paul may have used $\theta\epsilon\acute{o}\varsigma$ of Christ. If there had been a song of praise to the Father here, it could have been a

---

[15] $\nu o\mu o\theta\epsilon\sigma\acute{\iota}\alpha$ occurs only here in the New Testament. In the LXX it occurs at II Macc. 6:23; IV Macc. 5:35; 17:16. Gutbrod (*Kittel* [*G*], IV, 1082) holds that in Rom. 9:4 (cf. 3:1 ff.) Paul refers to the law, not the giving of the law; but in its context the latter sense is more probable, since that context concerns God's gifts. The giving of the law at Sinai is differently treated in Gal. 3:19-20 and II Cor. 3:7-18.

[16] The promises are closely linked with the succeeding term, "patriarchs," and with the preceding, "covenants," which God made with the early figures of *Heilsgeschichte*. For the use of the word see *Billerbeck*, III, 206-08, where material has been collected from the LXX, Josephus, and the pseudepigrapha; a more thorough collection from these sources is to be found in *Kittel (E)*, II, 576-80 and in Bauer-Arndt-Gingrich.

[17] $o\acute{\iota}$ $\pi\alpha\tau\acute{\epsilon}\rho\epsilon s$ can apply either to the wilderness generation (I Cor. 10:1) or to the patriarchs: Abraham, Isaac, and Jacob. Cerfaux, *op. cit.*, p. 25 (*Recueil Lucien Cerfaux*, p. 362) says rightly, "There is no need to ponder over Romans 9:5; it can be taken to mean the three great patriarchs."

[18] See N. A. Dahl, "Die Messianität Jesu bei Paulus" (*Studia Paulina, Festschrift J. de Zwaan;* Haarlem: de Erven F. Bohn N. V., 1953) pp. 83-95.

[19] See especially *Sanday and Headlam*, pp. 233-38; F. C. Burkitt, "On Romans IX 5 and Mark XIV 61," *Journal of Theological Studies*, 5 (1904), pp. 451-55; C. Lattey, "The Codex Vaticanus on Romans IX 5," *The Expository Times,* 34 (1922/23), p. 331; C. Lattey, "The Codex Ephraemi Rescriptus on Romans IX 5," *The Expository Times*, 35 (1923/24) pp. 42-3; L. G. Champion, *Benedictions and Doxologies in the Epistles of Paul,* (Heidelberg, 1934) pp. 124-46; Lucien Cerfaux, *Christ in the Theology of St. Paul*, translated by Geoffrey Webb and Adrian Walker (New York: Herder and Herder, 1959) pp. 517-18; and *Michel,* pp. 197-99.

customary Jewish doxology added to the enumeration of the mighty works of God. This, however, would seem out of place in a context that deals with God's gifts and their rejection by unbelievers. As it stands, the passage makes better sense if it applies to Christ. With this mention of him and his relationship with Israel according to the flesh, the dominating theme in the salvation history of his chosen people has been sounded—right at the beginning of Paul's treatment of the Israel problem. In his own person Christ links the old covenant with the new. He is God over all, also over Israel, to which he belongs on the human side (κατὰ σάρκα). This is restated, a little differently, in Rom. 10:12: ὁ γὰρ αὐτὸς κύριος πάντων, πλουτῶν εἰς πάντας τοὺς ἐπικαλουμένους αὐτόν. Christ, the judge at whose wrath Israel and all who love it must tremble, is of the people of Israel, and at the same time God over all, both over Israel and over the Gentiles. Therefore these words, so promising for what comes after, are followed, not indeed by a doxology, but by an expression of praise, the first portent of the subsequent redemption of Israel through Christ and an anticipation of the praise of 11:33-36. Here is implicit not only the statement already quoted—Romans 10:12, that he bestows his riches upon all who call upon him, Israel as well as the Gentiles—but also the subject to be discussed immediately afterward, which is, in Paul's own words: "So whatever promises there are, they have their Yes in him" (II Corinthians 1:20).

It should be added that the expression chosen by Paul to describe Christ, ἐπὶ πάντων θεός, is offensive to the Jews, affronting their conception of what is meant by "one true God." But this is exactly where the ways part. The Jews do not believe in Christ as the Savior sent by God, while Paul affirms that only in Christ, and not by any self-elected way of salvation, is there salvation for all.

An earlier debate concerning Romans 9-11, which maintained that this whole section was an excursus, or a previously composed passage inserted after chapter 8 and before chapter

12,[20] can now be considered resolved for good. The assured result emerging from this discussion is that these three chapters deal with a problem fundamental to the earliest church, which if not correctly resolved will leave the whole import of the letter hanging in mid-air.[21]

## 9:6-13: God's promises have not lapsed because of the Jews' (present) state as outcasts from Christ; for the promises have never applied to all the descendants of the patriarchs, but only to those chosen by God.[22]

The unbelief of the Israel of Paul's day does not mean that the word of God (i.e., God's promises) has lapsed.[23] For God's promises to Israel did not give the Jews any claim upon God. The Jews cannot rely on their descent by blood from the patriarchs. They cannot maintain that they are the true Israel and therefore share in the advantages and merits of the patriarchs. Election depends rather upon the free mercy of God, as can be seen from Israel's earliest history, where God chooses one son of a patriarch and ignores another.

Underlying this problem is a decisive factor, namely that both Christianity and Judaism use the Old Testament as Holy Writ. The new religion saw in Christ's work and its own rise a fulfillment of God's promises in the Old Testament. Jews who did not believe the gospel would probably have opposed this view with the natural objection that these promises concerned the Jews and that their fulfillment in the Christian church could not be of God, since physical Israel had had no part in it. The unbelief of the Jews is not merely a missionary

[20] *Dodd*, pp. 148-50.

[21] *Nygren*, pp. 353-360.

[22] Cf., in spite of all the differences, *Kühl*, pp. 316-24.

[23] Cf. Flavius Josephus, *Antiquities*, II.219 (B. Niese, ed., *Antiquitates Judaicae*, 7 Vols., [Berlin, 1885-95] I, 128, 13). Moses' father, Amarames, feared: τοῦ θεοῦ τὴν ἐπαγγελίαν ἀφανίσειεν and II, 220 (Niese, I, 128, 17-18): τὸν δὲ θεὸν ἡγεῖτο πᾶσαν ἐκποριεῖν ἀσφάλειαν ὑπὲρ τοῦ μηδὲν ψευδὲς γενέσθαι τῶν εἰρημένων.

problem that concerned the earliest mission to the Jews, but a fundamental problem for all Christian thought in the earliest church. Israel's unbelief is a difficulty for all Christians, both Jewish and Gentile. If God has not fulfilled his promises made to Israel, then what basis has the Jewish-Gentile church for believing that the promises will be fulfilled for them? It must not be forgotten that this transference of Israel's promises to the Gentiles was not, at the time of the apostles, the simple matter that it has since become for the Gentile church. In Romans 9-11 we have Paul's opinion on this question. Like the earliest Jewish Christianity, he knows that the present unbelief is a fulfillment of the Scriptures, and he also agrees with Jewish Christianity in hoping for the early salvation of Israel,[24] but he differs from the earliest disciples of Jesus in conceiving the period before the salvation of Israel as one to be spent in mission activities among Gentiles. To the post-apostolic church, which did not share the first generation's view of Israel but had witnessed the fate of the Jews in the aftermath of their rebellion and viewed it as a punishment from God, it was natural to answer the question posed in 9:6: "Have the promises lapsed?" with, "No, for they have been fulfilled in us, the true Israel of God, the church of Gentiles, because the Jews have hardened themselves in their unbelief, and have thus already and irrevocably refused salvation." [25] It is important right from the start for us to realize that Paul, like the rest of early Christianity, differed decisively from the later Gentile church in his view of Israel.

Even though he maintains in this passage that God in his sovereign will chooses whom he wishes, one must not fail to

[24] Cf. Peter's speeches in Acts 2:22 ff.; 3:13 ff.; 10:37 ff.; cf. 13:23 ff.; James' speech at the apostles' meeting, Acts 15; and Paul's emphasis on Jews first and then the Greeks, Rom. 1:16; 2:9-10—a view which he is hardly alone in maintaining.

[25] For this reason the Gentile church takes over the Old Testament as its own, and regards it as no longer the holy scriptures of the Jews. Cf. I Clement and Barnabas. How early is this view in the church? As early as the speech in Matt. 28:18-20 when the disciples are sent forth? As early as the cursing of the fig tree, Matt. 21:18-22?

add: whom he wishes *from Israel*. Paul does not here visualize "Israelites" who do not belong to the physical Israel as being within the new Israel of the church.[26] It is not until 9:22 ff. that Paul includes the Gentile Christians in his reflections. Here in 9:6-13 the only point he makes is that claims cannot be made on the basis of physical descent, since descendants of the patriarchs with exactly the same claims were allotted different destinies.

What has happened in the time of Paul, that only some of the descendants of the patriarchs have come to belong to the true Israel while others have not been chosen, was anticipated in early times. Abraham was chosen to carry on the promise,[27] but none of his sons was given the promise on the basis of physical descent. Only Isaac was Abraham's seed,[28] for it is not the children of the flesh, but only the children of the promise, who are "reckoned as descendants."[29] In Galatians 4:21-31 Paul has treated Abraham's two sons, the children of Hagar and Sarah, again without mention of Ishmael by name. As in Romans 9:8, Paul distinguishes in Galatians 4:23 between the two sons of Abraham by saying: "But the son of the slave was born according to the flesh, the son of the free woman through promise." And in vv. 28-30 he proceeds to apply what has been said to his readers and his own time: "Now we, brethren, like Isaac, are children of promise. But as at that time he who was

[26] Thus *Maier* (p. 16 ff.) is correct: the note in 9:6-8 is altogether that of οὐ πάντες (p. 17). To which may be added that later, in 11:25-36, it is altogether that of πάντες (πᾶς 'Ισραήλ). See also *Althaus* (p. 86) on 9:9; also *Gaugler* (II, 23) who rightly protests against the interpretation of chapter 9, which holds that the promise is transferred from the physical to the spiritual Israel, namely the church. The promise has not lapsed with the rise of the church (cf. p. 24 f.).

[27] Abraham is here conceived as the father of the circumcised and not as father also of the uncircumcised (Rom. 4:9 ff.).

[28] Gen. 21:12, also quoted in Heb. 11:18. The word to Abraham in v. 9 is a combination of Gen. 18:10 and 14. The miraculous element in the birth of Isaac is stressed by Paul, Rom. 4:16-25.

[29] The rabbis do not include the Ishmaelites in the seed of Abraham, nor Esau in Isaac's seed; see *Billerbeck*, III, 265.

born according to the flesh persecuted him who was born according to the Spirit, so it is now. But what does the scripture say? 'Cast out the slave and her son; for the son of the slave shall not inherit with the son of the free woman.' " This new emphasis—that the patriarch's descendant who did not receive the promise persecuted the one who did inherit it—is not applied to Ishmael in Romans 9:7-9. He is not even mentioned by name. But the idea does show up in the succeeding passage concerning the sons of Isaac, and becomes a dominant theme from verse 14 on, making it quite natural to assume that the idea is implicit here in Romans 9:7-9.[30]

The same was the case with Isaac.[31] He was the child of promise, and was reckoned as a descendant, but his sons did not inherit the promise just because they were blood descendants.[32] Their case shows how God's choice of the true Israel is made. The two sons of Israel were twins, and the choice was made before birth when they had done neither good

---

[30] Cf. Rom. 4:16-22. *Lietzmann* writes, p. 91: "Verse 8 can actually be understood only by those who are already familiar with Galatians 4:21-31 and who know that Paul is using Isaac allegorically as a prototype of 'those who are justified by faith.' " The two events referred to in Rom. 9:6-13 are comprehensible only to those familiar with Genesis. Since discussion of the use of the LXX in the earliest churches continues, there is reason to draw attention to the degree of biblical knowledge which Paul assumed on the part of his readers, and to the fact that the natural basis for this is regular Bible reading during the service and possibly also in the home.

[31] πατήρ, cf. προπάτωρ of Abraham, Rom. 4:1.

[32] The circumstance that the son of promise is born of a hitherto barren wife, so heavily stressed in Sarah's case at Gal. 4:27 by the quotation from Isaiah 54:1, is also related concerning Rebecca in Gen. 25:21. That Rebecca was barren at first is also stated in *The Biblical Antiquities of Philo,* tr. M. R. James (London: SPCK, and New York: Macmillan Co., 1917) XXXII, 5, p. 175, with a curious departure from Genesis, "And to Isaac he gave two sons, which also were from a womb shut up, for at that time their mother was in the third year of her marriage." In Gen. 25:20, 26 it is related that Isaac was forty years old when he married and sixty when his two sons were born. It is natural to stress how the promise is continued by means of God's gracious intervention. Abraham and Isaac would have had no descendants if God had not acted. Thus the continued existence of the chosen people through the birth of new sons of promise is always dependent upon God.

nor evil,[33] but were, humanly speaking, equal before God.[34] God fulfills his redeeming will by choosing Jacob, and the choice is determined by God's call, and not by the deeds of the person called.[35]

Of Isaac's twin sons, the one chosen was proclaimed as such by God even before birth;[36] at still another point, however, this

[33] Later, on the basis of Gen. 25:22, "The children struggled together within her," the rabbis speculated as to what happened in the womb of Rebecca and at their birth, concluding that Esau even then attempted to take his brother's life, and acted ill toward his mother (*Billerbeck*, II, 528-29). Philo takes a more optimistic view of the twins when in the womb, *Legum Allegoriae III*, 88-89.

[34] *Weiss*, among others, rightly points out that this second example is not subject to the objection that could be raised against the first, namely that only Isaac was a legitimate son of Sarah. Rom. 9:11-12a is a parenthetical passage stressing the correspondence between choice by God and justification by faith. God's choice is not determined by the merit of the chosen.

[35] Paul's line of thought is the opposite of the Jewish idea expressed in Jubilees 15:30: "For Ishmael and his sons and his brothers and Esau, the Lord did not cause to approach Him, and he chose them not because they are the children of Abraham, because He knew them, but He chose Israel to be His people" (R. H. Charles, ed., *The Apocrypha and Pseudepigrapha of the Old Testament in English*, 2 Vols. [Oxford: Clarendon Press, 1913] II, 37.) In ecclesiastical exegesis this explanation appeared in the early church, as shown by *Bardenhewer*, p. 142. See Ambrosiaster (Migne, ed., *Patrologiae cursus completus: Series Latina*, 221 Vols. [Paris, 1844-66] Vol. 17, col, 141) and Chrysostom (Migne, ed., *Patrologiae cursus completus: Series Graeca*, 161 Vols. [Paris, 1857-66] Vol. 60, col. 555). Cf. K. H. Schelkle, *op. cit.*, pp. 20-25 for the relation between God's *praescientia* and *praedestinatio* according to the Fathers, and pp. 25-31 for their interpretation of Rom. 9:10-12. For their interpretation of the text see also the works listed above, p. 27, note 1. See also *Billerbeck*, III, 267, where rabbinical statements are cited which make the fulfillment of God's word in Gen. 25:23 dependent on whether the younger keeps the commandments and so on. In Mekilta (*Mechiltha*, trans. by J. Winter and Aug. Wünsche, [Leipzig, 1909] p. 208) there is a description of how God offers the law to the peoples, but only the Israelites will obey it. When the sons of Esau hear that it is written in the law, "Thou shalt not kill," they point out that their paternal inheritance is "By your sword you shall live" (Gen. 27:40).

[36] This was also the case with Isaac, but Ishmael had then already been born, Gen. 17:15-22. *Lietzmann*, commenting on Rom. 9:10, criticizes Paul's use of Gen. 25:23 in Rom. 9:12 because the Genesis passage speaks of two peoples, and not of two individuals. But to this it must be replied that Paul uses the quotation correctly because he is in fact in this passage speaking of peoples and not of individuals, as Lietzmann indeed subsequently notes.

second illustration used by Paul goes beyond the first. The insertion of the quotation from Malachi, "Jacob I loved, but Esau I hated," makes a sharp distinction between the son of promise and the son of the flesh, and Esau is referred to in a manner that anticipates the reference to Pharaoh in verses 14 ff. The name of Esau or Edom has associations differing from those of the unexpressed name of Ishmael (verses 6-8). Even in Genesis there is a decisive difference between the two pairs of brothers: Ishmael and Isaac, Esau and Jacob. Esau is Jacob's enemy; he seeks revenge for Jacob's appropriation of Isaac's blessing, even though the showdown never occurs.

In late Judaism Jacob's fear and Esau's thirst for revenge (as we know them from Genesis 27:41-45; 32:3-32; 33:1-16) are dramatized in the story of Esau's attempt to kill Jacob which is found in Jubilees 37-38 and Testament of Judah 9. The latter relates only the external circumstances of this battle: Jacob lays Esau low with an arrow and his sons pursue the sons of Esau, besieging them in their stronghold and imposing a tribute on them. In Jubilees, on the other hand, we are given a detailed account of the external and internal history of the clash. There is a description of Esau's hatred of Jacob, which leads him, urged on by his sons, to forget his oath to his parents that he would keep peace with his brother, and to attack Jacob in order to kill him. This bitter enmity is expressed in Esau's words to Jacob, which state clearly that it can never cease: "If the boar can change its skin[37] and make its bristles as soft as wool, or if it can cause horns to sprout forth on its head like the horns of a stag or of a sheep, then will I observe the tie of brotherhood with thee."[38] (One is reminded that in apocalyptic imagery Esau is described as a wild boar—a black boar, Enoch 89:12, cf. the reference to Esau's descendants in

[37] Cf. Jer. 13:23: "Can the Ethiopian change his skin?" In *Adversus Indoctum* 28, Lucian plays on a proverb: Αἰθίοπα σμήχειν ἐπιχειρῶ (cf. "Loeb Classical Library" [London, 1929-41] III, 208).

[38] Jubilees 37:20 (Charles, *op. cit.*, II, 69).

verses 42, 43, 66[39]—while Jacob and his descendants are described as sheep.) Then the battle begins, and Jubilees 38:2 describes the murder of Esau by Jacob (cf. Ezekiel 25:14, "I will lay my vengeance upon Edom by the hand of my people Israel"), while his sons destroy Esau's army and impose a tribute on the Edomites which perseveres to this very day.[40]

The background of this late Jewish story is to be found in the Old Testament accounts of Edom's conduct toward Israel, particularly when Jerusalem was destroyed by Nebuchadnezzar in 586 B.C.[41] According to Ezekiel 25:12-14, punishment will fall upon Edom because it has sought revenge upon the house of Judah. Therefore the Lord will destroy man and beast and make it desolate by the hand of Israel. Obadiah 10 prophesies that Edom shall be cut off forever because of "the violence done to your brother Jacob," and the succeeding verses tell in detail how Edom rejoiced at Jacob's destruction. Lamentations 4:21 likewise mentions that punishment will overtake Edom, while Psalm 137:7 beseeches: "Remember, O Lord, against the Edomites the day of Jerusalem, how they said, 'Rase it, rase it! Down to its foundations.'" The closest parallel to the late Jewish story is probably Ezekiel 35:1-15, where Ezekiel prophesies the destruction of Edom. Here too it is an eternal destruction, "because you cherished perpetual enmity, and gave over the people of Israel to the power of the sword at the time of their calamity." This "perpetual enmity" is a brief and

---

[39] On the swine used to symbolize Rome, see P. Volz, *op. cit.*, p. 280.

[40] While the battle and its conclusion—and also the place-name, Mount Seir (Jub. 38:9; Test. Jud. 9:3)—are largely the same in the two sources, the external circumstances differ in that according to Test. Jud. the sons of Esau shut themselves up in their stronghold after their father's death, while according to Jub. Esau and his sons and his army advance against Jacob, who lives in a tower on Mount Hebron (Jub. 36:20; 37:15 ff.).

[41] This is doubted by Max Haller, "Edom im Urteil der Propheten" in *Vom Alten Testament, Karl Marti zum 70. Geburtstag,* ed. K. Budde (*Zeitschrift für die Alttestamentliche Wissenschaft,* Beiheft 41, 1925), pp. 109-117, who admits that this hatred towards Edom did not exist before the Exile, but who then reduces the historical significance of the threatening passages by assuming literary dependence.

accurate rendering of Esau's words in Jubilees 37. In the *Heilsgeschichte* Edom's sin—trying to subjugate the covenanted land of Canaan and to destroy the covenanted people of Israel —results in God's decision to destroy Edom. In Ezekiel's words: "Because you said, 'These two nations and these two countries shall be mine, and we will take possession of them'—although the Lord was there" (v. 10), therefore Edom is now to acknowledge "that I am the Lord" (verse 15).

Because of Esau's attempt to attack the inheritor of God's promise—his own brother—and because of Edom's never-forgotten attempt to destroy the chosen people in their deepest affliction and to possess the promised land in spite of God's covenant and promises, the name Edom came to have a special association, living on as a typical designation for those hostile to Israel. In the changing history of Israel the name came to be applied to different peoples. Thus we find it used of Rome. According to a generally accepted interpretation "Esau" in IV Esdras 3:16 and 6:7-10 is Rome. "Edom" is the last empire; when it falls, Israel's kingdom begins, with no interval of time intervening. Earlier, according to Daniel 7:18 ff., the kingdom of Israel was to replace the Syrian kingdom, at that time treated as the fourth and last of the heathen empires.[42]

Thus we see that from the patriarchs are descended, side by side, both the true Israel and the power hostile to Israel and Israel's God, a power on some occasions interpreted as "Syria" and on others as "Rome."[43] In our present reference (Romans 9:13) "Esau" probably represents the physical Israel, which within the brief duration of the new covenant has threatened to take upon itself this resistance to God and his redeeming will.

[42] Cf. Volz, *op. cit.*, p. 380. For Esau (Edom) as Rome see *ibid.*, pp. 29, 280, 380 and *Billerbeck*, III, 81-2, 267-68.

[43] The Fathers trace the descent of the Antichrist through the tribe of Dan; see, e.g., Irenaeus, *Contra omnes haereses*, V, 30, 2; Hippolytus, *De Antichristo*, XV; and Pseudo Ephraim 6. Test. Dan 5:6 is the earliest testimony to the close connection between Dan and the Antichrist. One may also point out that Dan is omitted from the list of those of the twelve tribes of the sons of Israel who are sealed as servants of God in Rev. 7:5-8.

God's words have not been invalidated, for they do not apply to all who are descended from the patriarchs. As far back as the earliest days, God by a promise chose Isaac, one of Abraham's sons, to perpetuate the chosen people, while his elder brother Ishmael became the founder of an alien people, the Ishmaelites. And Ishmael even persecuted the son of promise.[44] Isaac's two sons by Rebecca suffer a similar fate. God selects the younger to be the founder of Israel, while the elder, Esau, becomes the founder of an alien people, Edom, which persecutes Israel to the extent that its name becomes the stock expression for Israel's chief enemy among the peoples.

Romans 9:6-13 is therefore speaking neither of individuals and their selection for salvation, nor of the spiritual Israel, the Christian church. It speaks rather of the patriarchs, who without exception became founders of peoples. God selected one son to carry on the chosen stock, but sent the other son away to become the founder of an alien people outside the promised land.

These events, familiar to every Jew and every Christian, show the acts of God as they are to be found even in Paul's own day. God's choice of a founder for his people is made in the midst of history and not before the creation. In the example of Isaac's sons, it is in fact emphasized that the word of promise was spoken before the two children were born in order that God's selective purpose might stand, based not upon deeds but upon him who called. This election does not presuppose predestination as commonly understood, a choice by God prior to creation. If that were the case, the time at which knowledge of the choice was made known would be of no significance. The announcement of the choice must be made immediately after the decision; God's choice is determined in the midst of history. God acts in history, decides, and—as we shall see—makes new

[44] Gen. 21:9 is thus interpreted in the rabbinical tradition (*Billerbeck*, III, 575-76). This interpretation was already put forward by Paul in Gal. 4:29.

decisions, because, while his intention of salvation stands, it is achieved by constant interventions into the changing circumstances of history.

As regards the history of beginnings related in Genesis, Paul has therefore emphasized that—like Israel—the surrounding peoples were descended from the patriarchs, but that they had not obtained the promise given to Israel. This parallels his own experience of the descendants of the patriarchs in Israel in their attitude toward Jesus and toward the apostles, including himself. Only a remnant have received the gospel. The others, for whom no word of promise has sounded, have turned away, and have given themselves to persecution.

## 9:14-18: God's choice cannot be termed unjust, since, as the examples of Moses and Pharaoh show, he chooses with sovereign might those to whom he will show mercy, and those whom he will harden.[45]

The principle that Paul in verses 6-13 has found in the *Heilsgeschichte,* namely that God chooses with sovereign might whomever he wills, to perpetuate the true Israel, raises the objection—presumably often encountered by Paul—whether this is not unjust. Here the patriarchs are not the objects of his concern, but men of his own time—the descendants of the patriarchs, of which the majority are skeptical toward the gospel and a minority, the "children of promise" are reckoned as Abraham's descendants. Behind the objection lies a Jewish idea that man's achievement within God's covenant of grace (the law) determines God's judgment upon him. But here God's judgment is passed independently of and prior to man's achievement. Can this be so? Is it not unjust? Paul answers by pointing out that God's procedure here is witnessed to in

---

[45] For the patristic interpretation which, as in the case of Rom. 9:10-12, explains Pharaoh's fate as his own fault, see K. H. Schelkle, *Paulus, Lehrer der Väter* (Düsseldorf, 1956), pp. 189-96 and the works mentioned above, p. 27, note 1.

Scripture, which says that God has mercy on whomever he wills. Therefore it cannot be said that Paul gives a negative answer to the question put in verse 14. Both here and later, Paul rejects the objections made by his opponents. It is therefore incorrect to designate the following passages as Paul's theodicy. A defense of God cannot be drawn up within early Christian theology, not even in answer to Jewish opponents. What has led earlier scholars astray in this context is the Jews' insistence that God cannot be unjust, on the basis of the Jewish view of the relationship between merit and fate,[46] and that Paul apparently accepts this Jewish view. It is evident, on the other hand, that the distinction between Paul and his Jewish adversaries lies in his refusal to measure God by human standards.[47]

God is sovereign in his saving acts, and human works provide no grounds for salvation.[48] Verses 14 ff. establish this as God's procedure. The word given to Moses[49] is a continuation of the examples of Isaac and Jacob: God chooses whom he wishes and it is not the will or the actions of man[50] but solely

[46] This is a frequently recurring subject in the New Testament, see Matt. 20:1-16. A Jewish corrective to the parable of the laborers in the vineyard is to be found in pBᵉrakoth 2, 5c, 15 (*Billerbeck*, IV, 1, 492-93).

[47] Cf. *Nygren*, pp. 365 ff. and *Althaus*, pp. 87 ff.

[48] The Jewish interpretation of the matter is to be found in the rendering of Exodus 33:19 (=Rom. 9:15) in the Jerusalem Targum: "I will spare him who is worthy to be spared, and I will show mercy upon him who is worthy of mercy" (cf. *Billerbeck*, III, 268). Rabbi Meir on the other hand employs this passage with regard to the question of why many sinners flourish in this life, in order to abandon any rational solution. God has not given Moses any answer to this question but (in Exodus 33:19) has pointed to his mercy, even for the unworthy (E. Sjöberg, *Gott und die Sünder im palästinischen Judentum* ("Beiträge zur Wissenschaft vom Alten und Neuen Testament," Vol. IV, No. 27), Stuttgart and Berlin, 1938, p. 111.

[49] In the opinion of *B. Weiss* (p. 412, commenting on v. 15) Paul stresses the fact that this word of God came to Moses because Moses in particular might be evidence that God's conduct toward men was determined by their conduct. To this it may be replied that Moses here represents not the law but the chosen people.

[50] Is Paul, when he says θέλω, thinking of Esau in Gen. 27:1-40, particularly v. 38? Cf. Heb. 12:17, θέλων and Josephus, *Antiquities* I:274 (Niese ed.,

God's mercy that decides whether the *Heilsgeschichte* shall be carried on through one part of a people or another, for this is a matter of peoples and parts of peoples, and not of individuals;[51] God chose Jacob (Israel) and not Edom. Nor is Moses conceived of as an individual; he here represents Israel, whom God chooses and saves in its affliction in Egypt. Over against Moses stands Pharaoh,[52] an adversary who like Ishmael and Edom is a threat to the continuance of the *Heilsgeshichte.* But God's sovereign will also rules Pharaoh, the representative of Egypt.[53] For this reason the conduct of God's adversary toward Israel is made to serve two purposes: (1) God wishes to demonstrate his power over Pharaoh in his vain opposition to the liberation of God's people, and in his fatal attempt to cross the Red Sea, the event which is more than any other a sign of God's choosing and saving of his own people. (2) The other way in which Pharaoh becomes part of the message of salvation is through his defeat, because thereby the name of God is reverenced throughout the earth. A woman who anointed Jesus in Bethany (Matt. 26:6-13; Mark 14:3-9) was promised that her action would be remembered wherever the gospel was proclaimed in the world. Pharaoh is even far more closely linked with the tidings of God's salvation, because by his opposition he gives God a victory to proclaim throughout the earth. His relationship to this salvation, however, is only as the adversary of God, and this also by God's decree. For while

I, 65, 23): ἠξίου. τρέχω designates an exhausting effort to press onward (*Bauer-Arndt-Gingrich, Bardenhewer*) and therefore presumably refers to the Jew's striving for righteousness through law (cf. Rom. 9:30-31; 10:2-3).

[51] Martin Dibelius in *Paul*, ed. by W. G. Kümmel and trans. by Frank Clarke (Philadelphia: Westminster, 1953) p. 34, differs with this. Rom. 9:15, says he, refers to a choice of individuals.

[52] *Lagrange*, p. 234, rightly says, "To Moses, as an example of grace, Paul adds the case of Pharaoh his adversary, who is a type of all those who resist God and refuse to obey his commands."

[53] *Kühl*, p. 325, *Lagrange,* pp. 233-234, and *Maier,* pp. 35-36, correctly conceive γάρ in v. 17 as forming a parallel to γάρ in v. 15 so that the accusation of ἀδικία is doubly rejected.

the words spoken to Moses in verses 14-16 (from Exodus 33:19) serve to establish that God chooses to show mercy according to his own will, the words to Pharaoh in verse 17 show that God not only extends mercy to whomever he wills, but also hardens whomever he wills (9:18).

This statement has been the subject of much discussion in the commentaries. The ἐξήγειρα quoted in Romans 9:17 corresponds neither to the Hebrew text nor to the LXX of Exodus 9:16. *Kühl* suggests alternative renderings of ἐξεγείρειν: "I have allowed you to appear in history," or better: "I have called you into being."[54] This distinction is certainly a modern one; the Old Testament line of thought, both regarding the conduct of the Gentile peoples and regarding the appearance of the prophets in the *Heilsgeschichte*[55] only concerns itself with the fact that these persons were summoned to a task in the saving history. *Sanday and Headlam* render the word: "raise up on the stage of history," and point to Habakkuk 1:6; Zechariah 11:16; Jeremiah 27:41, all in the LXX.[56] It is used of the Gentiles in Habakkuk 1:6 (LXX); II Chronicles 36:22; II Esdras 1:1; cf. Isaiah 41:2 (LXX: δικαιοσύνην); Jeremiah 6:22; 27(50):41.[57] *Bardenhewer* assumes that ἐξεγείρειν must mean more or less the same as σκληρύνειν but this assumption derives from his belief that the content of 9:18b must be a recapitulation of the quotation in verse 17. Since this is not necessarily so,[58] his assumption is not at all self-evident.

---

[54] *Kühl*, p. 325: "geschichtlich auftreten lassen" and "ins Dasein rufen."

[55] See PSM, p. 29.

[56] *Sanday and Headlam*, p. 256.

[57] The simple ἐγείρω is used in the LXX for "causing to appear in *Heilsgeschichte*": Judges 2:16, 18; 3:9, 15; I Kings 11:14, 23; Isaiah 41:25; 45:13. The verb is also used in this sense in the New Testament for God's intervention in redemptive history, in some instances weakened, as, "to be raised up," Matt. 3:9; Luke 3:8; Matt. 11:11; 24:11, 24; Mark 13:22; Luke 1:69; 7:16; John 7:52; Acts 13:22.

[58] God's hardening of Pharaoh's heart is indicated in Exodus 9:12 just before the passage quoted here, in addition to all the passages cited in Note 61 below. σκληρύνω is used of Pharaoh in Exodus 4:21; 7:3, 22; 8:15; 9:12, 35; 10:1, 20, 27; 13:15; 14:4, 8, 17.

Another issue often brought up, and closely connected with God's intention in raising up Pharaoh, seeks a solution by "posing the correct question"—not "How is mankind saved?" but "How does God work in history?" Such an approach has a modern ring to it. A historian has no answer to such questions unless the ancient writer himself was in some position to formulate and weigh them and, by setting down his answer or his reflection, to give us some enlightenment concerning them. And that would presuppose a philosophico-theological doctrine of predestination that Paul, with his idea of God as the one who saves Israel and the Gentiles by intervening in the course of history, could not possibly have held.

We must first of all put the question whether Pharaoh is here regarded as an individual or as a representative of the Egyptian people. For Pharaoh is the third example of the non-chosen who persecutes the chosen people and—like the first two examples, Ishmael and Edom—could reasonably be thought of as representing a people, the Egyptians. If in this context he must represent an individual, then he would have to be a particular Egyptian king. Pharaoh stands as a figure of Antichrist, who appears at a decisive point in the *Heilsgeschichte* and attempts to exterminate the chosen people. Israel's delivery from Egypt is, of course, a type of the eschatological liberation. Moses, or a man like him, is awaited as the leader in an approaching crisis of salvation.[59] It is therefore necessary, in the

[59] Cf. Adolf Schlatter, *Das Alte Testament in der johanneischen Apokalypse,* (Beiträge zur Förderung christliche Theologie, Jahrgang 16, n. 6; Gütersloh: C. Bertelsmann, 1912), p. 84: "Just as the deliverance from Egypt is a sign and prototype of the future redemption, so also the manner in which Pharaoh is chastened and humbled is symbolic of the manner in which God will someday humble and chasten mankind. The prophetic interpretation of the Egypt-figure comes from the tradition: 'All the plagues that God brought upon Egypt he will also bring upon Edom, upon this godless Rome' (Tanchuma בא 6) by which is meant that a parallel is to be sought for each of the Egyptian plagues in the prophecies directed against Edom and Gog. John [the Revelator] is not bound by any such rigid system, nevertheless this basic idea —that Moses' struggle with Pharaoh prefigures the end time—is what guides him also." Cf. Volz, op. cit., p. 370; *Billerbeck,* I, 756-58; and Joachim Jeremias in *Kittel (G),* IV, 861, 2-28.

context of Romans 9:22, to interpret the passage concerning Pharaoh eschatologically. (See below for the parallels between the two passages.) The reference here is to the coming salvation of the true Israel and to the power that is trying to prevent it—the power which once was Pharaoh and is now the physical Israel, bent both on persecuting the church and on trying to hinder its preaching of the gospel to the Gentiles.

In the history of salvation there are persons chosen by God for key roles. Abraham in the Old Testament and Paul in the New Testament are examples. But there are also negative figures in the *Heilsgeschichte*, of whom the greatest is Antichrist. These figures enter into the sacred history as individuals who have a special task in the struggle against God in the latter days. When in the present instance I reject such an interpretation, and assert that to Paul Pharaoh signified the Egyptians—the people that persecutes God's people and tries to destroy it—my position is based partly on the treatment of Pharaoh in late Jewish texts, and partly on the text of Romans 9.

Admittedly, Josephus contains two expressions where Pharaoh acts as an independent individual. In *Antiquities* he writes of Pharaoh: Φαραώθης δὲ οὐ τοσοῦτον ὑπὸ ἀφροσύνης ὅσον ὑπὸ κακίας ὅμως αἰσθόμενος γὰρ τῆς αἰτίας ἀντεφιλονείκει τῷ θεῷ καὶ τοῦ κρείττονος ἑκὼν προδότης ἐγένετο. And he renders Exodus 10:3 as: ἄχρι πότε ἀπειθεῖς τῇ τοῦ θεοῦ γνώμῃ.[60] These psychologizing versions are typical of the writer Josephus, but hardly of the Jewish tradition he received. In Exodus Pharaoh is an expression of the attitude and will of the Egyptian people.[61] How this portrayal could be interpreted in

[60] Josephus, *Antiquities* II. 307, 309 (Niese ed., I, 147, 19-21 and I, 148, 10-11).

[61] God hardens Pharaoh's heart: Exodus 4:21; 7:3; 8:19; 9:12, 16 (quoted, Rom. 9:17); 10:1-2, 20, 27; 11:9, 10; 14:4, 8, 17-18; cf. Exodus 7:13, 22; 9:7, 35. Exodus 7:14 is merely a confirmation that Pharaoh's heart is hardened, while 8:15, 32 and 9:34 speak of this hardening in the passive: he was hardened. The Egyptians are referred to as Pharaoh's people: Exodus 8:29, 31 and 9:14, 16. They shall know that "I am the Lord," 7:5; 14:4, 18, by the fact that God leads his people out of Egypt against the will of that

late Judaism can be seen in Philo,[62] who describes the exodus from Egypt without any mention of Pharaoh, except in two opening lines that correspond to Exodus 1:8. In Philo, Egypt is a favorite symbol of the body and the passions. Pharaoh is mentioned separately, characterized especially as ὁ σκεδαστὴς τῶν καλῶν,[63] but it cannot be said that Pharaoh appears as an independent factor side by side with Egypt. He merely represents his country, with the special significance attributed by Philo to Egypt. In I Clement 51:5 it is likewise Pharaoh and his army and all the princes of Egypt who have hardened their foolish hearts. Irenaeus argues with some who maintain that God has hardened *cor Pharaonis et famulorum eius*; in his own words it becomes: *Pharaonem, cum his, qui cum eo erant.*[64] According to *Billerbeck*[65] the rabbis have not devoted much attention to Pharaoh. The material mentioned here provides no basis for the assumption that Paul adopted an interpretation of the Pharaoh figure that could have led him to see it as a manifestation of Antichrist.

Nor does the text lend itself to such an interpretation, when no precedent existed for it in contemporary Judaism. Pharaoh in his hardened and persecuting conduct is compared to the physical Israel, and it is therefore quite natural to suppose that he represented the Egyptian people, to whom the Jews were a counterpart in Paul's scheme of things.

## EXCURSUS 1. ISRAEL AS PERSECUTOR

It is common to recognize Israel's unbelief, but not to see its hardening, and the concrete expression of that hardening: persecu-

country. In Exodus 14:17 it is actually stated, "I will harden the hearts of the Egyptians." Even the fact that God gives Israel favor in the sight of the Egyptians, Exodus 3:21; 11:3; 12:36, is only a further proof that God controls his opponents with sovereign power.

[62] Philo, *Antiquities,* X (James, *op. cit.,* note 32) pp. 103-06.

[63] *De Sacrificiis Abelis et Caini* 48 (Cohn and Wendland, I, 221, 12).

[64] Irenaeus, *op. cit.,* IV, 29, 1-2.

[65] *Billerbeck,* III, 269.

tion. An account has already been given above of the way in which
the non-elect son of the patriarch persecuted the son of promise.
Pharaoh and Egypt are not of the chosen people, but they represent the power hostile to God and the chosen people. Just as God's
purpose was to show his power through Pharaoh, and thus make his
name proclaimed throughout the earth, so his purpose now is to
show his wrath and make his power known. He will make known
the riches of his glory on the vessels of his mercy: the church made
up of Jews and Gentiles (verses 22 ff.). The resemblance between
Pharaoh and the physical Israel of Paul's day consists in the latter's
enmity toward God and its effort to destroy those who have in-
herited God's promises according to his will. As a parallel to this,
we have in 10:9 Paul's emphasis on the confession of the mouth
as well as the belief of the heart, which, as pointed out by *Pallis,*
should be interpreted as confession before the authorities. In 11:2 ff.
Paul compares himself to Elijah. The prophet had come from his
exile among the Gentiles in Zarephath to the test of power on Mount
Carmel in order to try to turn his people to God and away from
their unbelief and persecution of the prophet's followers.[66] Similarly, Paul, while writing his letter to the Romans, is preparing
for his journey to Jerusalem with the collection. This gift to the
poor of the church in Jerusalem has significance for a wider circle
than these needy Christian Jews. In order to present the collection,
Paul will bring along representatives of the Gentile churches that
have taken part in the collection. Thus Israel will see representatives
of the Gentile peoples who have received the promises spoken in
connection with Israel, but which the chosen people still refuse to
see as fulfilled in the God-given Messiah who has brought in the
beginning of the last times. Again in 11:28 we hear, for the last
time, of the Jews' hostility toward the Christian Gentiles; as regards
the gospel, the Jews are hostile for the Gentile Christians' sake.
And later, in chapter 15, Paul asks the Roman church to strive in
prayer with him that he may be delivered from the unbelievers in
Judea, a request that is elucidated and confirmed by the description
in Acts 21-28. The decisive argument for interpreting Romans 9-11
as dealing with Israel not only as hardened in unbelief, but also
as in hardness of heart persecuting the chosen Israel of the church,
is to be found in chapter 8. As early as 5:3 it is stated that we not

[66] See above, pp. 108-09.

only exult in the hope of God's glory, but also in our sufferings, because we know that suffering trains us to endure, endurance brings character, and character hope. Here persecution is introduced as a basic Christian theme, which is not a surprising theme to hear from the author of the two letters to the Corinthians. Romans was probably composed less than six months after II Corinthians, whose basic theme is that suffering is normal for a Christian, in contrast to the worldliness of the Corinthians who shrink away from suffering for the faith. In Romans 8 the theme of suffering again appears, not as the main theme of the passage, but as a subsidiary theme which still makes itself heard in the midst of the description of the Christian life and its glory. We know from II Corinthians that the Christian's glory and his suffering are indissolubly united. The further we advance into chapter 8, the more the ideas of suffering and persecution are mixed with the rejoicing. This begins at 8:17 (8:11 is uncertain), where there is a close parallel to Galatians 4:7 (as there are parallels in the preceding passages of both letters), but at this particular point only Romans contains the addition: "provided we suffer with him in order that we may also be glorified with him." And the next verse continues this theme: "I consider that the sufferings of this present time are not worth comparing with the glory that is to be revealed to us." The following verses are not concerned with suffering, and the subject does not recur until nearly the end of the chapter. After having stated in vv. 28-30 that God having begun the good work will also finish it, Paul asks: "If God is for us, who is against us?" And when this question has been answered, he asks: "Who shall separate us from the love of Christ?" Here he lists first of all the tribulations of the apostolic life, especially persecution.[67] After this Paul quotes Psalm 44:22, "For thy sake we are being killed all the day long; we are regarded as sheep to be slaughtered." This text from Psalms, applied by the rabbis to the Jewish martyrs of the Maccabees period,[68] is taken by *Lagrange* to refer to the worst that could happen rather than to events that had

[67] θλῖψις is often used elsewhere by Paul, together with στενοχωρία, Rom. 2:9; II Cor. 6:4; the corresponding verbs and also διώκω in II Cor. 4:8-9. διωγμός is used together with θλῖψις in II Thess. 1:4 and together with στενοχωρία in II Cor. 12:10. κίνδυνος is used several times in II Cor. 11:26, where λιμός and γυμνότης are used in v. 27.

[68] *Billerbeck*, III, 259.

recently taken place. *Holtzmann* and *Althaus* rightly point out that Paul is referring to experiences that are still being endured. *Dodd's* comment is very much to the point: "There is a peculiar pathos about some of the items in this list. Paul was writing on the eve of his last voyage to Jerusalem. He was putting his head into the lion's mouth, as he well knew (cf. Acts 20:22-25)."[69]

There remains the question whether *Dodd* and *Michel* are right in emphasizing the personal element so strongly that the words become a description of the apostle's experiences rather than a picture of the circumstances of the churches at the time Paul was writing. While Paul in his two letters to the Corinthians speaks of his own apostolic sufferings as a model for that church, which up to that time had avoided suffering and hoped to continue avoiding it (though not in the period between the two letters, according to II Corinthians 1:6-7), there is no reason in the letter to the Romans to limit the suffering so as to apply only to the apostle. The "we" used by him embraces the Christians in general. It is true that it has caused some surprise that Paul should speak in this way at a time when there were no persecutions on the part of the authorities. If, however, we assemble from our sources in the New Testament all that we know about persecutions of the church at this time, the words appear neither theoretical (expressing in concrete terms the thought in 8:17b) nor exaggerated. The passage refers to the Jews' persecution of Paul, of the Gentile Christian churches founded by him, and of the Jewish Christian churches in Palestine.

Naturally Paul, as a Christian Jew and a leading missionary, was persecuted more than his more humble Gentile fellow-Christians, who as natives of the different cities might also be less accessible to attack by Jews, who were not in a position everywhere to start a persecution without running a risk themselves. Since we know much more about Paul than we do about his churches, we must, from the amount we know about the apostle, deduce an evidently lesser degree of persecution as regards those churches, even though we are not without information that they were persecuted.[70]

Even in Damascus after his conversion and call, Paul was persecuted and in danger (from the Jews, according to Acts 9:22-25; Paul himself speaks of King Aretas' governor, II Cor. 11:32-33).[71]

[69] *Dodd*, p. 146.

[70] We know of persecution in Thessalonica from I Thess. 1:6; 2:14; II Thess. 1:4; in Corinth from II Cor. 1:6-7. Cf. Gal. 3:4.

[71] Cf. PSM, p. 203, note 1.

The same thing happens on a later visit to Jerusalem, where the "Hellenists" try to kill him, but the brethren get him away and send him to Tarsus (cf. Acts 9:29).[72] Next time we hear of Paul in detail is in Acts 13-14, the account of the first missionary journey. Here, at Antioch of Pisidia, he finds that the Jews will not allow the Gentiles to hear the gospel, and this results in a breach between him and the synagogue. A little later the Jews here start a persecution against Paul and Barnabas, forcing them to leave the district (Acts 13:50). Something similar occurs in Iconium, where the unbelieving Jews in the synagogue stir up the Gentiles against the apostles and force them to flee (14:2, 4-6). And when work is begun in Lystra, Jews come from Antioch of Pisidia and Iconium, win over the crowd, and stone Paul (14:19). On the second journey Paul is thrown into prison at Philippi although not at Jewish instigation (16:16-40). His troubles in the next cities, however, are all brought about by the Jews. In Thessalonica it is the jealousy of the Jews that gives rise to the disturbances which in the absence of the apostles affect their host, Jason, and certain other Christians (17:5-10).[73] Jews from Thessalonica, on hearing that Paul is now preaching in Beroea, come to this town and stir up trouble, again forcing the apostle to resume his journey (17:13). While there is no persecution in Athens, although Paul is indeed examined before the court of the Areopagus, we find in Corinth the usual series of events: Paul first preaches in the synagogue, but the attitude of the Jews forces him to break with them (18:4, 6). Later the Jews bring Paul before Gallio's court, but are unable to get him convicted (18:12-17). On the third journey the same thing happens in the synagogue at Ephesus as occurred in Corinth (19:8-9). The later persecution in connection with the silversmiths' great demonstration was not instigated by the Jews (19:23-40). The obscure episode of the Jews and Alexander (19:33-34) could be interpreted,

[72] Lyder Brun, *Segen und Fluch im Urchristentum*, pp. 127-28, thinks that the reality behind Rom. 9:3 is that Paul was cursed by the Jews. N. Månsson, *Paulus och judarna* (Uppsala: Almqvist & Wiksell, 1947), pp. 125-26, together with note 58 on p. 239, holds that we can safely assume that Paul was under the ban of the synagogue.

[73] The use of συμφυλεταί and 'Ιουδαίοι in I Thess. 2:14 seems strange when this text is approached via Acts 17. Is this text, like Acts 9:22-25, an example of Luke's tendency always to blame the Jews? Or is Paul speaking of a persecution after his departure and Luke of a persecution (by the Jews) that ended in his departure?

as suggested by Lake and Cadbury,[74] as meaning that the meeting in the theatre looked as if it might develop into an anti-Jewish "pogrom." The fact that the Jews in the other cities could win over the crowd shows that their position had been so consolidated that subsequent disturbances would not recoil on them. But we know from Paul himself and from another passage in Acts that the Jews on other occasions persecuted Paul in Ephesus; this is Paul's speech to the elders of Ephesus in Miletus, 20:18-35, where the apostle in verse 19 speaks of the "tears and . . . trials which befell me through the plots of the Jews." Paul's fight with "beasts" at Ephesus (I Corinthians 15:32), and the danger of death in Asia to which he refers in II Corinthians 1:3-11, may possibly be references to the same event, but they cannot apply to the uprising of Demetrius as recounted in Acts. On the other hand, the two Pauline texts might naturally refer to the persecutions, or one of the persecutions, to which Paul was subjected in Ephesus at the instigation of the Jews. The reference in II Corinthians 1:3 ff. indicates that it was no ordinary danger but something especially deadly.

This picture of the Jews as persecutors is confirmed by Paul's letters, where, in II Corinthians 11:24, 26, we read that five times Paul received from the Jews "the forty lashes less one," and that among the various hardships was "danger from my own people." In I Thessalonians 2:14-16 the Jews are described as in opposition to all men, in that they hinder the apostles from speaking to the Gentiles that they may be saved. Presumably Galatians 5:11 (cf. 6:12) must also be taken to refer to persecution on the part of the Jews.

Apart from Paul's letters and the accounts concerning Paul in Acts, we hear of Jewish persecution of the Christians in Acts 1-12: after the healing of the lame man at the temple gate Peter and John are seized and imprisoned (4:3-21). Later all the twelve apostles are imprisoned (5:17-41). In 6:12—7:60 an account is given of the persecution and death of Stephen. The succeeding general persecution of the Christians (8:1, 4 ff.; 11:19 ff.) is described in Acts as the cause for the spread of the gospel through the preaching of the fugitives in those places where they sought shelter. But Paul's reference to his participation in this persecution,

[74] F. J. F. Jackson and K. Lake (eds.), *The Beginnings of Christianity*, Part I, *The Acts of the Apostles*, Vol. 4 (English translation and commentary by Kirsopp Lake and Henry Cadbury, London: Macmillan, 1933) p. 249.

in the speech before King Agrippa (26:10-11), shows that Luke knows from the tradition he took over that punishments and torture were used, and that in several cases a sentence of death was passed. Agrippa I had the apostle James beheaded and Peter imprisoned, and only a miraculous delivery from prison saved the latter from death (12:2-19). Apart from Acts we learn in Josephus of the execution of James, the brother of the Lord, as a Christian martyr.[75]

Furthermore, we know from the Synoptic Gospels that those circles that handed on the gospel material suffered from persecution, and it is unnatural to regard so established an element in this tradition as having arisen later as a result of the persecution by Rome. More probably were Jesus' words about persecution preserved and developed from early times by the Jewish Christians in Palestine because of persecution by unbelieving fellow-countrymen.[76]

The old notion of an initial period free from persecution succeeded under Nero by continuing persecution on the part of Rome, must therefore give way to the conception that the church was persecuted from the beginning, first by the Jews, who did so partly through their own courts or by bringing charges before Roman courts, and partly by rough and ready means such as murder, and later by the Roman state. The transition to this later period is perhaps also due to the Jews, for the action against Paul seems to be intended to draw the attention of the Roman authorities to the fact that Christianity is not a Jewish sect but a new religion which, like any new oriental religion, was not covered by the law.[77]

## 9:19-21: If God both shows mercy and hardens hearts it seems as if he cannot blame men, but Paul dismisses this objection, and points to God as the supreme arbiter of mankind.[78]

Again an objection is raised to Paul's description of God's

[75] *Antiquities* XX, 199-203 (Niese ed., IV, 309, 22—310, 16).

[76] Texts such as Matt. 5:10, 11-12; Luke 6:22-23, 27. Matt. 10:16-39; Mark 13:9, 11-13; Luke 12:2-9, 11-12; 21:12-16; 12:51-53; 14:26-27; 17:33. Matt. 16:24-28; Mark 8:34—9:1; Luke 9:23-27. Matt. 23:29-37; Luke 11:47-51; 13:34. Matt. 24:9-13; Mark 13:13; Luke 21:17-19.

[77] Cf. PSM, pp. 317-19.

[78] See Schelkle, *Paulus, Lehrer der Väter*, pp. 196-201, for the interpretation of Rom. 9:20 ff. found in the Fathers.

sovereign will.[79] Guilt and responsibility must necessarily be excluded because God can blame no one, since no one can escape his will whenever he decides to harden a heart. If there is to be guilt and punishment, man must have the possibility of doing or not doing. Therefore, it is objected, what Paul says cannot be true.[80] Again, as in verses 14-15, Paul rejects the actual questioning as wrong. Men are always guilty before God and dependent on his mercy, irrespective of whether he shows mercy or hardens their hearts. It is by faith only, without works, that men are saved. And this is God's procedure throughout the *Heilsgeschichte,* that he sovereignly saves or allows to be lost.

In an earlier passage Paul has already referred to this problem, which the Jews at once pounce upon when confronted with the doctrine of righteousness by faith without works. In 9:14 he dismissed the idea that it was unjust of God to choose Jacob, and pointed to the testimony of Scripture that God shows mercy to whom he will, even as he later stated that God likewise hardens whom he will. And as far back as 3:1-8 Paul put forward this problem in a passage that anticipates many of the questions in chapter 9. In 3:1 Paul asks what advantages the Jew has, and mentions as the first that they have been entrusted with the oracles of God (verse 2). His next question anticipates a central idea in chapters 9-11 with the words, "What if some were unfaithful? Does their faithlessness nullify the faithfulness of God?";

[79] For the form of the objection see *Pallis* on 2:1; H. Almqvist, *Plutarch und das neue Testament* ("Acta Seminarii Neotestamentici Upsaliensis," XV), Uppsala, 1946, p. 87.

[80] Paul's immediacy can be seen from the fact that a few exegetes forget that their task is to give an account of Paul's ideas and begin to protest. Thus *Jülicher,* p. 296: "We can fully appreciate the authority of the potter in verse 22; he is doing no one an injustice—but applying this to God causes some serious difficulties." Of the power of the potter over the clay *Dodd* remarks, "It is a well-worn illustration. But the trouble is that a man is not a pot; he *will* ask, *'Why did you make me like this?'* and he will not be bludgeoned into silence. It is the weakest point in the whole epistle" (p. 159).

and likewise the answer, "By no means! Let God be true though every man be false," in accordance with Psalm 51:4: "That thou mayest be justified in thy words, and prevail when thou art judged" (verses 3-4). This seems to imply that the unbelief of the Jews cannot nullify the faithfulness of God and make his promises to Israel empty and invalid. The faithfulness of God ought thus to be the guarantee that he will save his disobedient people. It is true that actual conditions are quite different. Here it is the Jews' unrighteousness that dominates the picture. But if this human wickedness proves that God is righteous, is it then just of God to let his wrath fall upon these wicked (verse 5)? Such a remark could be made only by one who measures God by human standards. And one may not speak like that, for one thing is certain—that God will judge the world, and therefore the righteousness of God is beyond any doubt, and the judge must be able to punish as well as acquit (verse 6). But is there not a connection between my lying and God's truth, so that the latter grows and abounds and gives him greater glory? What about this negative function? Is it not a positive function which ought from this point of view to prevent my still being judged a sinner? And can we not from this conclude further, as some impute to us: "Let us do evil, that good may come"? But Paul refuses to argue with such opponents. The whole of this elaborate construction and distortion of the declaration of justification by faith is to him evidence that such men are properly under judgment by God (verses 7-8).

Thus Paul has never answered these objections made by his opponents. He may point to the testimony of Scripture, which is of course valid both for Jews and for Christians (9:14 ff.), and he may refuse to discuss God's injustice by stating that God will judge the world. In other words he may reduce the objection to what is for both Jews and Christians a cardinal and undiscussable point of dogma, with the result that the objection falls to the ground. Here in 9:19-21 he dismisses the objection that the all-powerful God can no longer blame those whom he has hardened, with a reference to the familiar biblical image of the potter's power over the clay. The potter is an image of God as creator: he shapes the clay according to his will, and makes vessels for beauty and vessels for menial use. The image is taken from the Old Testament, where it is used in Isaiah 29:16; 45:9; Jeremiah 18:6 (cf. Isaiah 64:8);[81] and Job 10:8-9. The image should not be interpreted as referring to the Creator's shaping of individual human beings; it is used rather in political and *heilsgeschichtliche* contexts, where God is dealing with the Gentiles and the chosen people. We find this expressed most clearly in Jeremiah 18:6-10: "O house of Israel, can I not do with you as this potter has done? says the Lord. Behold, like the clay in the potter's hand, so are you in my hand, O house of Israel. If at any time I declare concerning a nation or a kingdom, that I will pluck up and break down and destroy it, and if that nation, concerning which I have spoken, turns from its evil, I will repent of the evil that I intended to do to it. And if at any time I declare concerning a nation or a kingdom that I will build and plant it, and if it does evil in my sight, not listening to my voice, then I will repent of the good which I had intended to do to it." This is exactly how Paul speaks of God's attitude to Israel in Romans 9-11: God decides in the various situations, although in Romans admittedly by grace and not by works. In Isaiah 45 the potter image (verse 9) is followed by an interpretation (verses 11-13): "Thus says the Lord, the Holy One of Israel, and his Maker:

[81] Another text cited in connection with this passage, Wisdom of Solomon 15:7 ff., does indeed contain the image of the potter who has power over the clay, but it is not used concerning God. This text belongs to another line of Old Testament tradition, that of the idols formed by craftsmen, a line which appears in Isaiah 40:19-20. Sirach 36 (33):13 deals with the Creator's attitude to individual beings. Concerning vessels for beauty and for menial use, see also II Tim. 2:20-21. NB: The chapter and verse numbering of certain Old Testament books differs in the Hebrew and Greek (LXX) versions. When such a situation occurs in this volume, the LXX numbering will be given first, followed in parentheses by the numbering used in the Revised Standard Version, which usually reflects that of the Hebrew text.

'Will you question me about my children, or command me concerning the work of my hands? I made the earth, and created man upon it; it was my hands that stretched out the heavens, and I commanded all their host. I have aroused him (i.e., Cyrus) in righteousness, and I will make straight all his ways: he shall build my city and set my exiles free, not for price or reward,' says the Lord of hosts."

To the Jews the hardening of Pharaoh's heart presents no problem. Even in the Old Testament God is sovereign in directing the history of salvation. Israel's history and the history of the world are directed by God, but with Israel alone as the goal of both. For instance, God summons the Assyrians to punish the kingdom of Judah (Isaiah 5:25-29), but afterwards God punishes the King of Assyria for his pride (Isaiah 10:5-19). Similarly, Pharaoh is merely God's instrument for chastening the chosen people and preparing its salvation. He is of no value in himself and is not an object of God's mercy. It is not until the church takes over the Old Testament that Pharaoh acquires interest as more than an instrument for God's dealings with Israel, becoming the representative of a people who also participate in God's salvation.[82] But the real interest that is attached to Pharaoh, as far as Paul is concerned in his opposition to the Jews, lies in the fact that Pharaoh's situation corresponded exactly to that of the physical Israel of Paul's day. God's people is on its way from Egypt to the promised land as was once the physical Israel (I Corinthians 10:1-13). And its adversary in Paul's day was the physical Israel, with its un-

[82] It is strange to read in Philo that "Egypt," where found in the Old Testament, signifies the body and the passions. Philo lived in Egypt perhaps all his life. About two hundred years later there lived in the same Egyptian city a Christian philosopher, Clement of Alexandria, who had learned extensively from Philo. He had so much to relate of Egypt that a whole book has been written on the subject: A. Deiber, *Clément d'Alexandrie et l'Egypte*, (Cairo, 1904; Paris, 1905). Philo and Clement differ in that the latter was a man of broad interests while the former in his writings expounded the Old Testament monotonously and abstractly; nevertheless, the difference in attitude toward the country and the people is fundamentally a question of religion.

belief and hardness of heart as expressed in its persecution of the church which is the true Israel.

One is thus compelled to ask whether the hardness of heart, spoken of here and evident to all who see Israel in its opposition to God, is regarded as anything other than a passing condition. This question is necessary, since Paul when writing of this is already aware of what we read in Romans 11, that God will save the whole of Israel. In that case all the dealings described in chapter 9 will be of limited duration. We read what is only too true in Paul's own time, and we must understand that God has the right to do what he will with his gifts. But when we read on, we are told that God does not show mercy and harden at will. Rather, his mercy is boundless, and even the aim of his hardening is mercy. The horror of the present situation will prove to be a portent of salvation for Jews as well as for Gentiles.

This glimpse of future events must, at the same time, not lead us to minimize the seriousness of the present state of affairs. To do that would be to regard the suffering church militant as though it were the *ecclesia triumphans*.

## 9:22-24: God desires to show his wrath, but has shown patience toward those destined for punishment, and thus has made his name known throughout the earth, allowing the gospel to be received by some of Israel and by the Gentiles.

In preceding passages (9:6-21) Paul has maintained that the Jews cannot claim anything from God as a right, but that God according to his will lets his promise to Israel be fulfilled for a part of the physical Israel. God shows mercy to the true Israel and hardens the heart of Pharaoh, the adversary of God's people. God has the right to do as he will with his own, and man has no right to measure God by human standards. But, Paul continues in 9:22 ff., what if God, desiring to show his wrath and to make his power known, as he did to Pharaoh (cf. verse 17), were to endure the vessels of wrath, in order to make known the riches of his glory for the vessels of mercy, namely those of us whom he has called—not from the Jews only but also from the Gentiles? Then no one would have the right to protest against God's all-powerful dealings.[83] Thus will the name of God be proclaimed throughout the earth. Here, then, we have the actual state of affairs. Paul dwells no longer on the fact that not all Jews are the children of promise, but points to the more promising circumstance that God has called some of the Jews and, in addition, some of the Gentiles.

It was necessary above to dwell in such detail on the figure of Pharaoh because the expressions used in Exodus about God's dealings with Pharaoh are here used about God's activities in the eschatological period during which Paul lived. But since all comparison includes resemblance as well as difference, it is necessary to try to determine the meaning of the expressions concerning Pharaoh in their topical application. Unfortunately, Paul's statement in verses 22-24 is no mere grammatical imperfection; it is also too brief to be interpreted with any degree of certainty. It is clear that the apostle is here saying something new, as compared with the preceding passage, and we are surprised not to find a simple statement that the chosen are to be glorified and the rejected punished. The new element now introduced is that God continues in his intention of showing his wrath and making known his power—he will still judge and punish—but that his working in *Heilsgeschichte* before the judgment is to have patience toward the vessels of wrath, although they are fitted for destruction, his aim being to make known the riches of his glory for the vessels of mercy, whom he is preparing for the glory to come, by calling the new Israel of the church not merely from the people of Israel but from

[83] This grammatically impossible construction concludes the argument of the preceding passage and brings us back to the actual state of things. Cf. Günther Bornkamm on Rom. 9:22-24 in *Das Ende des Gesetzes* (2nd ed.; Munich: Kaiser, 1958) pp. 90-92.

the Gentiles also. If this interpretation is correct, there are many details in these three verses that require closer consideration.

First of all, we must ask what Paul means by God's intention of showing his wrath and making his power known. This double statement is keyed into the scriptural quotation about Pharaoh in verse 17, by using ἐνδείξασθαι to correspond to ἐνδείξωμαι and τὸ δυνατὸν αὐτοῦ for τὴν δύναμίν μου. It is therefore reasonable to assume that the two elements of verse 22 correspond to the single element of verse 17 (ὅπως ἐνδείξωμαι ἐν σοὶ τὴν δύναμίν μου), the more so because God's power is revealed to Pharaoh by the plagues of Egypt and by the loss of the Egyptian army in the Sea of Reeds.[84]

By this wrath, which is postponed but not canceled out, may be meant (1) a special punishment inflicted on the unbelieving, persecuting Jews, stress being laid, if so, on the close correspondence between the physical Israel of Paul's day and Pharaoh and Egypt in Exodus. In I Thessalonians 2:16 there is mention of a special punishment of the Jews through God's wrath: ἔφθασεν δὲ ἐπ' αὐτοὺς ἡ ὀργὴ εἰς τέλος. This difficult passage has given rise to different interpretations, according to whether ἡ ὀργὴ is regarded as eschatological wrath or as a wrath or punishment from God that has already appeared in this world. ἔφθασεν has been regarded as the past, or interpreted as the future; εἰς τέλος can likewise be expounded in different ways.

(a) If ἔφθασεν is taken as a prophetic aorist,[85] similar to

---

[84] It is worth noting, with reference to the succeeding γνωρίσῃ τὸν πλοῦτον τῆς δόξης αὐτοῦ, even though it is not decisive for the understanding of v. 23, that God in Ex. 14:4, 17, 18 (cf. Eze. 28:22; 38:23) says, ἐνδοξασθήσομαι ἐν Φαραω. The significance of δόξα is of course not the same in Rom. 9:23 as the same stem in the verb ἐνδοξάζω in Exodus, but the question is whether Paul has entirely severed the connection with the text in Exodus, or whether he is deliberately using expressions which are reminiscent of the Pharaoh episode but which point in the opposite direction.

[85] Suggested by E. von Dobschütz, *Die Thessalonicher-Briefe* ("Kritisch-exegetischer Kommentar," 7th ed.; Göttingen: Vandenhoeck & Ruprecht, 1909) pp. 115 f. One might mention the rule given by Clement of Alexandria, derived from Pantaenus, that prophecy expresses itself indeterminately, and

the many aorists that the LXX uses to describe future events, the passage is reminiscent of prophecies regarding the destruction of Jerusalem found in the first three Gospels. The addition of εἰς τέλος, however, makes the pronouncement absolute: wrath has fallen upon them "completely" or "forever." In this case the passage is not compatible with the view in Romans 11, which presupposes the ultimate salvation of the Jewish people. Anyway, it is difficult to believe that ἔφθασεν is a "prophetic aorist," since such an application of the aorist is not found elsewhere in the New Testament.

(b) If the words are understood as a single, complete sentence of punishment upon Israel, a punishment that has already taken place, then there is reason to interpret this—since events that could give rise to such a pronouncement are hardly to be found in Paul's own day—as referring to the destruction of Jerusalem in A.D. 70, and to assume that the words are a later addition to Paul's letter by a reader who had experienced this event.[86]

(c) ἔφθασεν (but better: ἔφθακεν) could be interpreted as past tense, signifying the hardening of the Jews that has already taken place, the effects of which continue (perfect tense). It could also mean the hardening of the Jews as a completed action in the past (aorist). In both cases a difficulty occurs: the wrath has begun in the past, but the time when it began is difficult to fix, since the Jews' persecution of the messengers of God extends from the prophets under the old covenant up to the present missionary work of Paul and the other apostles. It is probably most reasonable to assume that the wrath, namely the hardening of the Jews, set in when they rejected the gospel of the crucified Messiah, before their attempts to prevent the Christian preachers from addressing the

uses the present tense for the future and the present tense for the past. Clement modifies this rule to interpret ἔθετο in Psalm 18:5 (19:4) to make it apply both to the past and to the future (*Eclogae propheticae* 56, 2-3).

[86] Cf. Luke 21:23-24, ὀργὴ τῷ λαῷ τούτῳ.

Gentiles. The persecution carried on by the Jews is therefore a symptom of their hardening, and this hardening is radical (εἰς τέλος). In this case the I Thessalonians passage is compatible with the view in Romans 11, where the hardening has already taken place, and no reference is made to the future.

(d) Lastly, one might consider whether εἰς τέλος in the New Testament has not acquired a new significance, extending beyond the ordinary Greek examples ("completely") and those in the LXX (also "forever"), because τὸ τέλος has become a term for the end of the world (Matthew 24:6, 14; Mark 13:7; Luke 21:9; I Peter 4:7; cf. Hermas, Visions 3, 8, 9).[87] The expression εἰς τὸ τέλος may therefore mean "to the end," i.e., until the last events at the end of the world. Thus mention is made of the endurance of the faithful "to the end" in Matthew 10:22; 24:13; Mark 13:13; cf. Revelation 2:26; Hermas, Similitudes 9, 27, 3. Now, the conversion of the Jews, as we can see in Romans 11:25-26, is in fact to be among the final events at the end of the world. If we venture to interpret the words of I Thessalonians 2:16: "Wrath is come upon them to the end," this passage makes the same statement as Romans 11. One difficulty remains: Paul in I Thessalonians, as shown by the concise form, assumes that his readers are familiar with what he in Romans 11 describes as "a mystery," but there is no decisive objection to this possibility. In the one case Paul is addressing one of his churches, which according to II Thessalonians 2:6 "now" knows what is left untold, while in Romans he is *inter alia* writing to a church with which he is not acquainted, and in which he cannot assume a knowledge of this secret.

In dealing with an idea of this kind—of God's wrath falling upon the Jews—one might assume that Paul, in Romans 9-11 and I Thessalonians 2:16, is influenced by common New Testament conceptions of a judgment upon Israel due to its rejec-

[87] τέλος is also used concerning the end of the life of Jesus, John 13:1; cf. Matt. 25:58.

tion of Jesus as the Messiah. The idea of such a judgment is to
be found in the words of Jesus to the women of Jerusalem in
the story of the Passion, Luke 23:27-31, which end with the
reflection: "For if they do this when the wood is green (viz.
crucify Jesus), what will happen when it is dry?" (viz. with
Jerusalem and its inhabitants). Jerusalem has let its opportunity go by (Luke 19:41-44). Reference may also be made to
the scene in Matthew where Pilate washes his hands and lays
the responsibility for the death of Jesus upon the people. The
people answer, Matthew 27:25, "His blood be on us and on
our children." Paul may remember such ideas, but only to reject
them. He does not draw the same conclusions as others concerning the unbelief of the people, but retains the authentic
early Christian belief that Israel will be saved.[88]

(2) Another possibility would be that by this "wrath,"
Romans 9:22, Paul meant the eschatological revelation of
wrath which will fall upon all. If Paul imagined the eschatological events to be as they are described in the Synoptic apocalypse (Matthew 24), i.e., that the incidents at the end of the
world are to be centered on the destruction of Jerusalem,[89] the
words here mean that God will bring the world and its center,
Jerusalem, to an end, but that he shows his longsuffering by
delaying in order that the gospel may be spread. Unfortunately, since we know very little about Paul's eschatology,
neither do we know if he connected the destruction of Jerusalem with the salvation of the Jews. Those passages in *Billerbeck* (I, pp. 876 f., 927; III, pp. 286, 289) which speak of
the repudiation of Israel and which might therefore be held to
reflect views familiar to Paul, do not refer to an eschatological
repudiation, but rather to Israel's repudiation and the elevation
of the Gentiles to become the political and military powers in
this world. Baruch 4:30 f. can distinguish between the destruction of Jerusalem and the salvation of Israel, but this passage

[88] See below, pp. 114-16 in regard to Paul's use of Psalm 69.
[89] Cf. Luke 21:23-24.

is possibly later than the Romans' destruction of the city in A.D. 70.

Thus the eschatological revelation of wrath in Romans 9:22 f. may apply to the Jews alone, taking effect in their obduracy, 10:21 and 11:7-10, so that God, as with the Gentiles, 1:19 f., punishes the sin of the Jews with sin. This is the interpretation of *Kühl* and *Maier*.[90] On the other hand, the wrath may mean God's general judgment, in which the Jews are included.[91] This would overcome the difficulty raised by Romans 11, where it is stated that the Jews are to be saved. If God is only delaying his wrath, then it cannot be aimed solely at the Jews. It must be assumed, therefore, that God is storing up an eschatological wrath, but plans in the meanwhile to save all Israel in the last days.

As in the scriptural quotation concerning Pharaoh, God intends to show his wrath and make known his power, but what is new and strange is that in his great forbearance he has delayed his punishing judgment, and has instead had patience with the vessels of wrath, who are fitted for destruction. Also, he has done this with an intent to save, for the sake of the new Israel, the church. With these words Paul not only returns to the actual state of things, but describes God's activities as they have concerned Christ and the events connected with his ministry. The day of the Lord and the coming of the kingdom of God have been postponed. Those who were fitted for destruction have been spared for the present. God calls vessels of mercy both from Israel and from the Gentiles and prepares them for his glory. This description in the aorist tense portrays events that have happened and are still happening. What is

[90] The interpretation of God's wrath as the obduracy of the Jews can of course also be accepted without the assumption made by these scholars that the hardening is the punishment for the Jews' unbelief. Cf. below on Rom. 9:30—10:21, pp. 75ff.

[91] ὀργή is used of the wrath of God which will be revealed at the end of the world, Matt. 3:7; Luke 3:7; Rom. 2:5; 5:9; I Thess. 1:10; Rev. 6:16, 17; 11:18; 14:10; 16:19; 19:15.

described here is the New Testament *Heilsgeschichte* up to the writing of the letter to the Romans.[92]

The words about God's endurance toward the vessels of wrath might still refer back to Israel's exodus from Egypt. They would then point to God's forbearance toward Pharaoh during the various phases of Moses' struggle to lead his people out of Egypt, until by the Sea of Reeds he let punishment overtake the vessel of wrath—Pharaoh himself, and his hardened people, who had long been ripe for destruction. If so, the words would in their topical application refer to the physical Israel, in its hardness of heart and persecution of the church, with whom God exercises patience because he intends salvation for Israel. Another possibility—and this seems the most plausible interpretation—is to take the words as applying to all peoples, stating that God's just punishment of the vessels of wrath is delayed with great patience in order that he may save the vessels of mercy. In both cases it must be assumed that the existing church of Jews and Gentiles mentioned in verses 23-24 is not the only result of God's patience, but that "the full number of the Gentiles" and the salvation of all Israel mentioned in chapter 11 are likewise the fruit of God's patience.

Romans 9:22 speaks of vessels of wrath made for destruction, and verse 23 of vessels of mercy, which God has prepared beforehand for glory. Paul's use of the expression "vessel" derives from Old Testament references to the potter who makes vessels for honor and vessels for dishonor from the same lump of clay. But it may be questioned whether σκεύη here has the same significance as in verse 21. In Jeremiah 27(50):25 and in Isaiah 13:5 (Symmachus) we find σκεύη ὀργῆς αὐτοῦ[93]

---

[92] Cf. Acts 17:30 where the same line of thought may be assumed: overlooking the times of ignorance (i.e., on the part of the Gentiles), God now offers all men everywhere (i.e., Jews and Gentiles) a possibility for repentance, for he has appointed a day "on which he will judge the world in righteousness." There will still be a judgment, but a prior way to salvation has now been opened.

[93] *Septuaginta*, XIV, J. Ziegler, ed., Göttingen, 1939, p. 170.

used concerning the weapons of the Lord's indignation with
which, according to the first text, he destroys the land of the
Chaldeans and, according to the second, the whole earth. This
meaning would fit Pharaoh. He is just the sort of weapon of
indignation that corresponds to Ishmael and Esau; he is the
persecutor used by God for a redemptive purpose. If this interpretation of σκεύη ὀργῆς is chosen, it is natural also to interpret σκεύη ἐλέους in the same way, as weapons used by
God with which to show mercy.[94] In that case σκεύη does not
refer to objects of God's wrath or mercy, but to agents who
effect God's wrath or mercy. In this connection a peculiar feature of Paul's thought in Romans 9-11 may be noted, namely
that none of the participants in *Heilsgeschichte* are saved or lost
for themselves alone. The hardening of the one has as its redemptive motive the salvation of the other, and again, the salvation of the other leads the salvation of the first after all. It is,
however, scarcely possible to choose with certainty between
these two senses of σκεύη.

Commentators have been particularly interested in
κατηρτισμένα εἰς ἀπώλειαν, attributed to "the vessels of wrath,"
and the phrase ἃ προητοίμασεν εἰς δόξαν, which is added to
"the vessels of mercy." Some have held that this is a case of
predestination in the philosophical sense, and have pointed out
that the vessels of wrath were already destined by God for destruction, while the vessels of mercy had been prepared by God
beforehand (i.e., before the creation of the world) for glory.
It must, however, be replied that this preparation for destruction and glory has taken place, and continues to take place,
within the New Testament *Heilsgeschichte*. There is no question
of a predetermination before the beginning of the world, but

[94] Thus *Lyonnet*, p. 104, who, however, interprets σκεῦος ὀργῆς as "objets
de la colère divine." σκεῦος is used of Paul in Acts 9:15, σκεῦος ἐκλογῆς.
Antichrist is the son of the Devil and Satan's σκεῦος, according to Hippolytus,
*De Antichristo* 57. The Devil dwells in him who does evil, as in a ἴδιον σκεῦος,
Test. Naphtali 8:6; the Holy Spirit will rejoice in the σκεῦος in which it
dwells, Hermas, Mandata, V, 1, 1. See also *Billerbeck*, III, 271-72.

only by actions of God within the range of history that Paul is able to survey: the period of Christ and the apostles. What is stated here is described in detail in what follows (9:30—11:10). The revelation of the riches of God's glory (verse 23) does not take place before the Second Coming and the judgment, and the preparation of the vessels of mercy for glory is therefore something that takes place in Paul's own day. As suggested above,[95] Paul may be thinking of the eschatological events described in the Synoptic apocalypse—perhaps even as presently occurring, if the critical view of Israel espoused by certain Gentile Christians (cf. 11:17 f.) is taken into consideration. In that case, Paul would be saying here that the imminent judgment upon Jerusalem and all obdurate and persecuting Jews—an important part of the last judgment—has been postponed, and the time is now being used to call the new Israel. The gospel must first be preached to all the Gentiles (cf. Matthew 24:14). If so, the statement is limited to the salvation of the Gentiles only (apart from "the remnant") and it is not until later that Paul speaks of the salvation of all Israel.

The vessels of mercy which God has prepared for glory—actually, "prepared beforehand" or "is preparing for the coming glory"—are "us," whom he has called, not from the Jews only, but also from the Gentiles. That God has called some of the Jews (among Abraham's and Isaac's sons, for instance) goes without saying. The difficulty lies in the fact that many did not become sons of promise. But here, for the first time in our passage, the Gentiles are introduced into *Heilsgeschichte*. God's call is not only to these among the Jews on whom he has mercy, but also to those among the Gentiles on whom he has mercy.[96]

[95] P. 65.

[96] *Maier,* p. 72: "We find καλεῖν also used in this sense in 9:12 and 9:24. It is, so to speak, a technical term, denoting the practical effect of God's call of grace. Cf. 8:28." In I Thess. 1:4 (part of the oldest Christian document in our possession) Paul speaks of the election of the Thessalonians, thus applying to Gentiles the fundamental Old Testament prerogatives ascribed to Israel.

As already mentioned, Paul is throughout this passage speaking of peoples and parts of peoples, e.g., Israel, the Gentiles, and the remnant. God decides that one or the other of these categories within *Heilsgeschichte* is to hear and receive the gospel, or that they are to be hardened. God's actions do not exclude the actions of men, as in so much modern talk of determinism and indeterminism. We do not have here the material for an exposition of Paul's views upon this modern problem. The apostle rather speaks of God's purposes for men and of the actions of these men, in a way that suggests that these coincide, so that if one wished—although Paul does not here so wish—he could give a detailed account of man's disobedience and guilt. But the relationship between human guilt and God's purposes is not, in this instance, that men sin and God then punishes them by hardening them (as in Romans 1:18 ff.; II Thessalonians 2:10-12). It is scarcely possible to say how these two things accompany each other or coincide in Paul's thoughts.

It is clear that this passage does not put forward a philosophical doctrine of predestination. As elsewhere in the New Testament, God is portrayed too "anthropomorphically" to make possible a view of predestination with an abstract concept of the deity as its subject. This is best seen from the important line of argument used by Paul: God's promises have not lapsed because of the unbelief of the physical Israel. It is God's decision that only a remnant should (as yet) receive the gospel. By seeking a self-determined way to salvation the Jews have offended against Christ, and have subsequently had their hearts hardened against the apostles. God acts in *Heilsgeschichte*, and even though he is free to act as he wishes, he always takes account of the varying historical circumstances.

However strange it may sound, God's decision to harden these hearts is to Paul the solution to the early Christian problem of Israel's unbelief. This terrible difficulty—that the chosen people did not receive God's fulfilment of his promises, and that the Gentiles who did receive it had to ask whether they could be certain of attaining that ultimate salvation which even the chosen people, to whom it had been promised, could not in their unbelief achieve—has found its solution in Paul's conception of a God-ordained system of salvation and damnation, whereby Israel's unbelief becomes a step toward the salvation of both Israel and the Gentiles.

A logical systematization of Paul's ideas will show that he has devoted himself to only a few problems, namely, those that were problems to early Christianity and to himself as missionary. Any attempt to trace the apostle's views beyond what he actually discusses will easily lead to contradictions. Paul speaks in practical terms on topical questions, but has no intention of supplying abstract, timeless solutions to the ever-recurring problems of thought.

### 9:25-29. Quotations from the Old Testament describe the present situation, that (as yet) not all Israel will believe, but only a part, while the Gentiles will now experience God's love.[97]

Interpreters have frequently transgressed with regard to Paul's use of the Old Testament, sometimes letting him "quote" an Old Testament text, sometimes letting him merely "use Old Testament phraseology to express his own thoughts." This seems an arbitrary view of Paul's relationship to the Old Testament. The correct procedure is a serious treatment of Paul's use of quotations or whole phrases from the Old Testament as a deliberate quotation of biblical texts. His interpretation of these texts may be surprising, but instead of giving rise to criticism it should make the commentator sit up and pay attention. By taking his use of the Old Testament texts as an indication of his understanding of them, one may penetrate more deeply into Paul's relationship to the Old Testament. Paul was trained in

[97] Cf. *Lietzmann* on 9:24.

the rabbinical interpretation of Scripture, and he applies this method in a number of cases. When on occasion he goes beyond not only the rabbis' interpretation but also their method of interpretation, this is no accident; as a Christian and an apostle, Paul has a new understanding of revelation that governs every use of Scripture in his letters.

**9:25-26** gives scriptural proof for καὶ ἐξ ἐθνῶν in verse 24. Hosea 2:1 is added to 2:23 (LXX, 2:25) because Paul wishes to say something new in relation to the quotation in verse 25.[98] This new item may be "sons of the living God," which to Paul may have sounded more telling than "my people" and "my beloved."[99] In the last line of the quotation from Hosea 2:1 there is an ἐκεῖ which may be an addition by Paul to the text of the LXX.[100] If this is the case, we must follow *Sanday and Headlam* in holding that this ἐκεῖ refers to Palestine since the Hosea text originally referred to the holy land. If this is what Paul means, we must assume that with this quotation, and his addition to it, he is referring to the gathering of the Gentile peoples in Jerusalem and the foundation there of the Messianic kingdom (cf. 11:26). *Sanday and Headlam* mention this possible interpretation with reference to the fact that Paul is often greatly influenced by the language, and even the concepts, of Jewish

[98] *Michel* (on 9:24) assumes that καλέω (v. 24) has determined the order of the two Hosea quotations which he (on 9:25 and 9:27 f.) holds to have belonged to a collection of quotations that existed before the letter to the Romans.

[99] Otherwise Paul does not speak of "children of the living God," but of "the children of God" or "the sons of God"; thus Rom. 8:14, 19; II Cor. 6:18 which is a composite quotation gathered from many Old Testament sources; Gal. 3:26; 4:6 (cf. Rom. 8:14-17); cf. Gal. 4:7. *Maier,* p. 56, writes of the expression "the living God," "For this very reason the idolatrous Israelites are a type of the Gentiles called during the eschatological age (*Heilzeit*), those who as Not-My-People used to serve idols but have now turned from that path to 'the living God' (I Thess. 1:9)."

[100] A. Rahlfs has this ἐκεῖ in the text of his short edition of the LXX (Stuttgart: Württembergische Bibelanstalt, 1935) while Ziegler in his edition of *Duodecim Prophetae, Septuaginta* XIII (Göttingen, 1943) p. 148 (on Hos. 1:10) does not include it.

eschatology, though in his more elevated pronouncements he seems completely emancipated from them.[101] In spite of this hesitation, *Sanday and Headlam* seem here to have hit on Paul's meaning, that it is in Jerusalem that the Gentiles are to be proclaimed children of God. This is in complete agreement with the significance elsewhere attributed by Paul to Jerusalem. At all events, this interpretation is far better than the other, also mentioned by *Sanday and Headlam*, according to which ἐκεῖ refers to the whole world: "Wheresoever on earth there may be Gentiles, who have had to endure there the reproach of not being God's people, in that place they shall be called God's people, for they will become members of his church and it will be universal."[102] This interpretation seems far less plausible than the former, which supplies an explanation for the heavy stress laid upon the place (ἐκεῖ) in the quotation, while the latter interpretation offers no such explanation.

And if this interpretation is correct, the reference to the proclamation of the Gentiles as sons of the living God in Palestine gives us exactly the new item that Paul wishes to add to Hosea 2:23 by linking it with Hosea 2:1. In Palestine the Gentiles will be acknowledged as children of God, it may be hoped, now, even at the conclusion of Paul's third journey, when the representatives of the Gentile churches travel up to Jerusalem with Paul, bringing their gifts.

**9:27.** There is no question of God's promises having lapsed (9:6); for the fact is that the present state of affairs, wherein only some of Israel will be saved, is prophesied in Isaiah 10:22 ff. Not Israel as a people, but only a remnant shall be saved. *Kühl* and *Boylan* hold that Isaiah 10:22 ff. is not a consolatory prophecy but an announcement of desolation: only a remnant shall be saved, as is evident from the preceding verses (20-21). This is partly true. "Only a remnant," is the tenor of

[101] P. 264.
[102] *Ibid.*

the whole continuum from verse 6 to verse 24, but verses 22-24 stress another thought: a remnant through mercy.[103] The same applies to the quotation in Romans 9:29, which is at one and the same time a threat of destructive doom and a promise of God's gracious deliverance from the threatened doom.

**9:28** is, like the conclusion of the quotation in verse 29, a biblical text concerning doom and destruction. Thus both statements confirm the statement of verse 22, that God will show his wrath and make known his power. This is so, but, say the quotations, a remnant of Israel shall be saved in addition to the Gentiles who are to be called his people.

How did Paul and those around him visualize this remnant? If we possessed chapter 9 without chapter 11, we could identify the remnant as the little group of Jewish Christians who in the Synoptic apocalypse flee out of Jerusalem (Matthew 24:16 f.), while all the remaining Jews are destroyed in God's judgment. But in the context of what follows it is natural to assume that the thought here is the same as in 11:1 f.: God has not completely rejected his people; there is still a remnant in the present church, that is, in the time between the Jews' refusal of the gospel and their ultimate salvation.

In **9:29** it is stated that it is solely through God's grace that a σπέρμα[104] (= ὑπόλειμμα in verse 27) has been left for Israel, so that its fate is not one of utter destruction, as in the case of Sodom and Gomorrha.[105]

---

[103] See below on 11:25, pp. 131 ff. Cf. *Maier,* p. 57 f.: "The apostle utilizes the characteristic wording of Isaiah's prophecy to demonstrate that even what seemed such an inconsequential thing as salvaging this apparently insignificant remnant of Israel had to take place, because the preservation of said remnant was directly willed and fulfilled by God—an act of divine deliverance as miraculous, a word of divine grace as pure, a wonder of divine mercy as great as any mass conversion of the Gentiles."

[104] Cf. σπέρμα in 9:6-13.

[105] The Jews of the day are compared to Sodom and Gomorrha in Matt. 10:15; Luke 10:12; Matt. 11:23-24; Luke 17:28-29. Rome is called Sodom in Rev. 11:8.

The Old Testament mention of a remnant is in Paul's day an assurance that God's promises have not lapsed. This concept of a remnant, which is a consolatory idea, concludes 9:6-29. It is taken up once more in 11:1 ff. In between, Paul deals with the Jews as a whole without mentioning that this remnant must be excepted.

## 9:30—10:21. The Jews' lack of belief in Christ.

Not until this point does Paul give a picture of what has happened to the Jews. Cf. above, on 9:1f. It is not correct to assume, as do nearly all commentators, that the preceding passage, 9:6-29, has viewed the casting-off of Israel from the aspect of the divine purpose, while Paul now, from 9:30 to 10:21, approaches the same question from the point of view of human responsibility. It is wrong because it is incorrect to assume that Paul shared the modern view that divine purpose and human responsibility are two separate parts of existence, which work independently of each other but which can be united if they can be made to agree with modern, anthropocentric ideas of divine justice.

Paul always seems to speak of election as something that has happened in history and is clearly evident in the world of experience.[106] There are visible fruits to show that God has elected (see I Thessalonians 1:4-5) but this election is not an irrevocable decision on God's part. Elected individuals may be handed over to Satan by church discipline (I Corinthians 5) and whole

---

[106] For ideas of predestination in late Judaism see G. F. Moore, *Judaism in the First Centuries of the Christian Era* (Cambridge, Mass.: Harvard University Press, 1932), I, 454-59, and J. Bonsirven, *Le Judaisme Palestinien au temps de Jésus-Christ* (Paris, 1934) I, 188-89, in the abridged edition translated by William Wolf, *Palestinian Judaism in the Time of Jesus Christ* (New York: Holt, Rinehart and Winston, 1964). I cannot, like K. G. Kuhn ("New Light on Temptation, Sin, and Flesh in the New Testament" in Krister Stendahl, ed., *The Scrolls and the New Testament* [New York: Harpers, 1957] pp. 94-113) find predestination or determinism in the Manual of Discipline (DSD 3:15-16), when this text is read in the context of what follows, especially 3:21-25.

churches may be excluded from Christ,[107] just as Israel and the Gentiles may be the objects of God's election or of his wrath. The life of mankind in history is subject to changes that prohibit a classical doctrine of predestination. Even "the apostle to the Gentiles," the chosen instrument who has been given a task of decisive importance to perform, must subdue his body and bring it into subjection, lest he who has preached to others should himself be a castaway (I Corinthians 9:27). Jesus has shattered the Jewish conception of a static predestination of Israel. Thus God has become all-powerful; he has mercy on whom he will, and hardens whom he will (Romans 9:18). But God's purpose of salvation—no matter what vicissitudes and unexpected turns it takes—is ceaselessly directed toward salvation.

This has been clarified for the church through Christ, in that, by means of this new light on God's will, the Old Testament can be read as God wishes it to be understood. One may speak of predestination insofar as God has earlier pronounced what is now to happen, but it is only in the light of Christ's ministry and his church's preaching of the gospel to Israel and the Gentiles that God's promises in the Old Testament are understood. Just as Jewish exegesis interpreted the Old Testament on the basis of that "present moment" concerning which it knew God had also spoken, so early Christian exegesis is an interpretation of Scripture on the basis of the great redemptive events presently being experienced.

Therefore God's purpose is at one and the same time pronounced beforehand in the Old Testament and yet something which happened yesterday, because it is only now that it has been concluded and proclaimed. In the light of that which has already taken place, which signifies a fulfillment of the Old Testament, Paul continues to labor to understand what the future will bring. His reflections are not theological in the sense that they express something universal and timeless. One understands these ideas better if he views their author as a

107 Cf. PSM, pp. 188-92.

missionary talking about his work—a work in which he is deeply involved. He knows the mission to the Jews quite as well as he knows the mission to the Gentiles, and in accordance with his custom he tries to penetrate behind present problems to the fundamental points of view. God's election is not an axiom but a fact which can be described, as Paul does in I Thessalonians 1:4-5. And behind this is God's purpose of salvation, of which he as an apostle, commissioned by God, feels himself to be an instrument. The unbelief of the chosen people is another fact willed by God, but presents a problem for all Christians in Paul's day, not only with its seeming contradiction of the Old Testament, but also with its apparent invalidation of God's plan of salvation.

The description that follows in 9:30—10:21 does not analyze the responsibility and guilt of the Jews. It merely catches us up on details of what has happened to the Jews, details not supplied us at the beginning of chapter 9 (or since then, for that matter). This banishment from Christ, the subject that so grieves Paul, and which he lamented in 9:3, is now described. In 9:30—10:4 we see the Jews' unbelief toward Christ, the promised Messiah, while in 10:5-21 we find an explanation of what the gospel contains after the death and resurrection of Christ, and how the gospel has been preached to the Jews by the apostles, though unfortunately in vain. At the same time, this passage explains the crux of the Jewish unbelief: by preferring a self-chosen way of salvation they have disobeyed God and have not followed the way he opened up in Christ—the way of faith, the only way to salvation. The passage concludes by giving a convincing impression of God's purpose: the salvation of Israel. First through Christ, whom they slew, and then through the apostles, whom they would not believe, he has held out his hands "all day long" to Israel (10:21).

It may be objected to this that the quotation just mentioned runs literally: "All day long I have held out my hands to a disobedient and contrary people," and on the basis of this and other passages (9:31-33; 10:2-3, 16) one could maintain that Israel's disobedience, and therefore its guilt, is what this passage aims to describe. The disobedience is of course mentioned, but if I quote 10:21 in a completely different context, I am only trying to stress that the emphasis is not upon Israel's disobedience, even though it fits naturally into the picture. The idea emerges most clearly if we compare Romans 9:30—10:21 with a text such as Stephen's speech in Acts 7:2-53. Stephen's speech also deals with God's redemptive relationship to Israel, and with the disobedience of the people to all God's emissaries. But while Stephen's speech is clearly an account of the disobedience and guilt of the Jews, and God's redemptive acts are mentioned only to provide a foil for Israel's constant resistance to God, the opposite is true for Paul's account in Romans 9:30—10:21. The Jews' disobedience and unbelief are mentioned, but without emphasis—merely as a fact. The core of the passage is God's way of salvation by faith, and His constant effort to make Israel hear and follow that way.

This view of 9:30—10:21 has the advantage of supplying an explanation of the second of the three sections into which Romans 9-11 naturally divides. If, like most commentators, we would regard this second section as a mere recapitulation of 9:6-29 from another point of view, or if we would consider it a kind of marginal comment, giving various facts about the problem in an interval between chapters 9 and 11, then the section would contain no advance in thought and have no organic place in the context. The case is different if by analogy with, e.g., I Corinthians 8-10 and 12-14 we regard Romans 9:30—10:21 as the heart of the message. We would then assume that the problem raised in 9:1-29 is here being solved without Paul having said, "Now I'm going to give you the solution." And chapter 11 would then be a detailed practical application of that solution. This fundamental and central section, then, serves to explain the way of salvation opened by God in Christ—justification by faith—and to make it clear that

God never tires of issuing the call to salvation, a call that includes Israel. As in the above-mentioned analogies from I Corinthians, the apostle seems at the beginning of the third section to refer back to the end of the first section, giving the impression that 9:30—10:21 is just a parenthesis; but it soon becomes obvious that, thanks to this middle section, the initial problems can be taken up in the final section and followed through to a solution.

## 9:30—10:4. The unbelief of the Jews toward Christ during his life on earth.

By human standards, it is paradoxical that God should give the Gentiles what the Jews strove for but did not attain to. It was Christ at whom they were offended. Israel pursued the law, which was to bestow righteousness but did not succeed in its purpose. This failure Paul explains as follows: Because (they sought it) not by faith, but as it were (ὡς) by the works of the law, they were offended at Christ, and crucified the Messiah. But he was that very stumbling stone that demanded faith, by which alone righteousness can be achieved. Israel's offence against Christ is expressed in Scripture.

9:30—10:4 is not concerned with the same subject as 10:5-21; it is concerned only with the earthly life of Jesus in Palestine, the Jews' rejection of him, and his crucifixion. References to this last event give Paul an occasion in 10:1 to pray for the salvation of the Jews, immediately after his terrible statement that Israel has crucified the Messiah. This reference also explains why Paul states in 10:4 that Christ is the end of the law, by his death on the cross. Not until after this indirect mention of the life and death of Jesus, and the consequences thereof, are the two factors in Paul's present situation stated, namely, what Moses says and what "justification by faith" says. Then follows the statement about the apostle's mission to the Jews throughout the world.

The quotation in 9:33 is composed of Isaiah 28:16 (also quoted in Romans 10:11) and Isaiah 8:14. It stresses that Jesus is the stumbling stone and at the same time the basis for salvation. As in I Peter 2:4, 6, 8, where these texts are also combined, there is here a reference to Christ as the cause of offense, rejected by men but dear to God, and therefore the cornerstone of salvation.

This interpretation of the Isaiah passage—making it refer directly to the death of Jesus—grows out of the New Testament practice of combining this text about the stumbling stone with Psalm 118:22. We find this in Luke 20:17-18 (where verse 18 adds, "Everyone who falls on that stone will be broken to pieces; but when it falls on any one it will crush him," which is also appended in several manuscripts to Matthew 21 as verse 44) and in I Peter 2:6-8. I Peter 2:4 has already alluded to Isaiah 28:16 and Psalm 118:23 ($\mathring{a}\pi o\delta\epsilon\delta o\kappa\iota\mu\alpha\sigma\mu\acute{\epsilon}\nu o\nu$ and $\pi\alpha\rho\grave{a}$ preceding $\theta\epsilon\hat{\omega}$). I Peter 2:6 quotes Isaiah 28:16, while verse 7 quotes Psalm 118:22. Verse 8 goes on to quote Isaiah 8:14, with the same wording as in Romans 9:33. I Peter 2 also has the Jews in mind, as indicated by verse 8, ". . . for they stumble because they disobey the word, as they were destined to do." Both in I Peter and in Romans this refers to the Jews; the later letter shares both texts and their exposition with Romans.

This statement, that God has set a stumbling stone and a rock of offence in Zion, is a way of saying that he acts as does the potter with his clay. He sets a stone which will cause the fall of many in Israel.[108] The Jews, who pursued righteousness, did not see what God did, but rather continued their eager pursuit and therefore stumbled at the stumbling stone, Christ, whom God had set in the midst of Zion to the end that he who believes in him will not be put to shame.

**10:1-4.** Israel, then, has rejected and crucified God's Mes-

[108] ". . . for the fall and rising of many in Israel, and for a sign that is spoken against . . ." are Simeon's words to Mary, Luke 2:34-35.

siah. After this has been stated in 9:30-33, Paul prays that they might be saved. The Jews have indeed ζῆλος θεοῦ[109]— here the concept ζῆλος is introduced, a concept which in chapter 11 acquires such decisive importance for the Jews in particular—but not κατ᾽ ἐπίγνωσιν.[110] They lack ἐπίγνωσις; indeed Paul can even describe them as ἀγνοοῦντες as far as God's righteousness is concerned. This does not apply to the Jews in Paul's present situation. They have both heard and understood (10:14 ff.).[111] But, as in 9:30-33, he is speaking of the Jews during the earthly life of Jesus. *Lagrange* writes: "ἀγνοοῦντες does not mean mere ignorance, since Paul has already charged the Jews (verse 19) with understanding all too well. Their problem is that they have *mis*understood."[112] But Paul is not speaking of the same thing in verse 3 as in verse 19. In the latter he is talking about the Jews' disobedience in defiance of the apostles' preaching of the gospel, but verse 3 concerns the Jews' ignorance of the Messiah as it relates to their disobedience toward him.

That the crucifixion was due to ignorance we know from another Pauline text, I Corinthians 2:8, "None of the rulers of this age understood this (i.e., the wisdom of God); for if they had, they would not have crucified the Lord of glory." We see in Acts that the Jews' rejection and crucifixion of the Messiah did not mean that they could not be saved. On the contrary,

---

[109] Cf. ζηλωτὴς ὑπάρχων τοῦ θεοῦ κτλ., Acts 22:3. The expression ζῆλος θεοῦ is found in II Cor. 11:2, ζηλῶ γὰρ ὑμᾶς θεοῦ ζήλῳ, where, according to L. J. Koch, *Fortolkning til Paulus' andet Brev til Korinthierne* (2nd ed., Copenhagen, 1927), it signifies God's jealousy as the spouse of the church (Israel).

[110] In Romans also at 1:28 and 3:20. Also in the prison letters, Phil. 1:9; Col. 1:9; 2:2; 3:10 and Philemon 6. In addition the word is used in Eph. 1:17; 4:13 and I Tim. 2:4; II Tim. 2:25; 3:7 and Titus 1:1 (in the Pastoral Epistles it is always stereotyped in the expression, ἐπίγνωσις ἀληθείας; so also in Heb. 10:26). The word also occurs in II Peter 1:2, 3, 8; 2:20—here used with a personal object (objective genitive), as in Ephesians and elsewhere in Paul.

[111] Cf. pp. 89-104 below.

[112] P. 253.

the apostles come to them, preaching the crucified but risen Lord; though the Jews in their ignorance have crucified Jesus, God has raised him, and now they are urged to repent and receive forgiveness for their sins. These three elements are found in several of the speeches in Acts—2:23, 36, 39; 3:13-14, 17-21, 26; 4:10-11, 27-28 (in this speech within the church the third element is lacking); 5:30; 10:36-42; 13:26-31.[113]

We also hear in the Gospels of the ignorance of the Jews, particularly in the account of Jesus' last visit to Jerusalem in Luke. Jesus weeps over Jerusalem, which does not know the things which make for peace, Luke 19:41-44, and he exhorts the women of Jerusalem not to weep for him, but for the un-suspected calamity that lies ahead, 23:28-31. And on the cross Jesus prays for his enemies (23:34): "Father, forgive them; for they know not what they do." Apart from this, Jesus' com-plaints over the Jews' or the disciples' lack of understanding generally allude to their lack of faith, their hard-heartedness, and their obduracy.

There is thus a difference between the interpretation of the Jews' lack of belief in Jesus found in Paul and Acts, on the one hand, and in the Gospels, on the other. Both Paul and Luke in Acts make the resurrection of Jesus the starting point for the preaching of the gospel to the Jews in particular, and this— only gradually, because of the lack of response—leads to an understanding of the obduracy of the Jews; the final form of the tradition contained in the first three Gospels shows that this obduracy is already evident among the Jews during the minis-try of Jesus in Palestine. Against this Synoptic background, it might seem that new campaigns by Jesus' disciples to win Israel would be superfluous, since they are doomed to failure from the start.

---

[113] Obduracy is also mentioned in Acts as a condition already existing among the Jews, 2:40; generally it is mentioned as something that does not emerge until the preaching of the gospel: Acts 3:26; 7:51-52; 13:41, 46, 51; 18:6; 19:9; 22:18; 28:24-27.

This difference can be explained in two ways. The Gospel tradition probably contains a reliable historical recollection of a powerful resistance to Jesus, described by him as obduracy. The resurrection then becomes the factor that gives the earliest church courage and hope to preach the glad message of the risen savior of Israel—even there where their master was rejected and crucified. The difficulty in this conception is that the earliest disciples, of whom we admittedly know very little, do not seem to have altered their master's message, but rather to have followed faithfully in his footsteps. A second explanation would be to assume that the disappointing results of the mission to the Jews, and the accompanying certainty of Israel's obduracy, expounded by Paul in Romans 9-11, is in the Gospels back-dated to the period of Jesus' life. In this case the great difficulty is that the unbelief and obduracy of the Jewish people are a fundamental theme of the tradition and could hardly have been introduced at a later stage, although it is possible of course that the already existing obduracy motif received its final form in the final redaction of the Gospels.

The Jews were ignorant of salvation in Christ, of that salvation which was won only on the cross—hence their ignorance during the earthly life of Jesus, which in Acts does not form a decisive bar to Jewish belief in the apostles' preaching of Jesus as the Lord who was raised by God from the dead. Because of this ignorance, and because of their attempt to find their own way to salvation, the Jews did not obey God's righteousness; that is, they did not obey Christ.

But when they had crucified him, Christ became "the end of the law, that everyone who has faith may be justified." It is by Christ's death on the cross, and the atonement thus gained, that an end is made once and for all to the law as the way to salvation (Romans 3:21-31; cf. Galatians 2:21; 3:13; Colossians 2:14; Ephesians 2:14-15). By the cross Christ has become the end of the law, so that there is now righteousness for all who believe.[114] This concludes the discussion of the life of Jesus, and Paul turns to an account of the apostles' preaching (note "we" in verse 8).

There is, here as in the preceding passage, no question of human guilt side by side with, or in contradistinction to, God's rule over mankind. The two things are interwoven without distinction.

## 10:5-13. The way to salvation opened by the death of Jesus: Justification by Faith.

We are now given an account of the Jews' self-appointed way to salvation, and of the Christian way to salvation, namely, justification by faith. The account in Galatians 3 helps us to understand that Christ really signifies the end of the Mosaic law. The two ways to salvation are so diametrically opposed that they exclude one another. To choose to follow the law in order to be saved leads to the curse, so that none can achieve righteousness and life in this way (Galatians 3:6-14).[115]

In my opinion *Maier's* interpretation of 10:5-13—concerning Israel's past, the time of Moses and the prophets, when Israel was prepared for the new way of salvation—is wrong. But he is right in his opinion that Paul is not trying in this passage to point out and prove the guilt of the Jews, but that throughout chapter 10 his aim is to show that God has done everything to win the Jews for the faith. Here something important is added that was not expressed in chapter 9. In that chapter it was established that God had adopted a remnant of

[114] *Gaugler*, II, 99 f., points to Niddah 61 b and thinks that further material for the conception found here—that the validity of the law ceases with the coming of the Messiah—would serve to show that Paul, with his message of justification by faith, is entirely within the realms of Jewish expectation. This overlooks the fact that the presence of the opposite conception among the Jews—that the kingdom of God and the law belong together—would in fact support Paul's view concerning the Jews of his day, namely, that they are attempting to put forward their own righteousness.

[115] Lev. 18:5 is quoted at Gal. 3:12 as well as at Rom. 10:5 (cf. also Luke 10:28).

Israel, as had been foretold in the Old Testament. But in chapter 10 it is shown that God has not ceased to call Israel, even though it has hitherto been disobedient. This prepares for the account in chapter 11 which shows that God is still working to save his people. Thus their present condition, and the Gentiles' reception of the gospel, are also part of God's plan for the imminent salvation of Israel.

10:5-8 describes the righteousness based on the law and the righteousness based on faith, both grounded in the Old Testament. Many commentators have not felt able to accept Deuteronomy 30:11-14 (expanded with Deuteronomy 9:4 and Psalm 107:26) as a scriptural quotation. Thus *Weiss* and *Zahn* maintain that the Old Testament words used by Paul are not a prophecy by Moses about justification by faith, but that Paul here uses words spoken by Moses to characterize the righteousness of faith. We find here the same tendency to distinguish between the use of authoritative scriptural texts, and the use of scriptural texts in formulating thoughts of one's own, as was previously discussed.[116] This tendency must also be dismissed here. It may more naturally be pointed out that what righteousness by faith "says" (10:6) is not given as a quotation from Moses, but is cited generally, as Holy Scripture. The pronouncement of law-based righteousness is by Moses, who here, as so often in the New Testament, represents the religion of the law. The case of the Deuteronomy quotation is otherwise. Here the righteousness based on faith is speaking. Only those so tightly bound to modern Old Testament scholarship and its complete perspicuity that they cannot dissociate themselves from it when investigating another period of history and its treatment of the Old Testament, are likely to object to Paul's use of Scripture here.[117] Paul's view of Scripture assumes that God

116 See pp. 71-72 above.

117 In dealing with Pauline quotations from the Old Testament, many commentators give a careful account of their context as viewed by present-day Old Testament scholarship. This has been deliberately omitted here, so

in the Old Testament has spoken of Christ and of salvation in him. The Jewish expounders of his day interpreted the Scriptures on the basis of events they had experienced. Similarly, God's dealings in history and God's words in Scripture seemed to go together in Paul's mind. History, he felt, provides us with a motive for searching God's words about what is happening now, while Scripture, in turn, throws light on all that has happened, explains God's underlying mind and will, and gives men cause for praising him. Just as the rabbis expounded the Old Testament according to everyday Jewish life of the period and the Qumran sect interpreted it on the basis of an eschatological period they were experiencing, so to Paul Christ is the key to everything written in the Old Testament, including the law. As Jesus in Matthew 19:1-12 (Mark 10:1-12) can retort with words from the creation account in Genesis 1-2 against the regulation about the bill of divorcement in Deuteronomy 24:1, describing the former as God's disposition and the latter as something that Moses permitted because of Israel's hardheartedness, so likewise Paul can here let the righteousness of law and the righteousness of faith speak through different statements from the Pentateuch. The closest parallel is to be found in Romans 4, where Abraham, the greatest of all the Jews, becomes in Paul's interpretation of Genesis the great example of the righteousness of faith, and thus also a father of the Gentile Christians.[118]

The interpretations added to the Old Testament words in 10:6-7 are either a polemical attack by Paul on the meaning

that readers will not be misled. It seems to me as unrewarding and obstructive to a proper understanding as if a scholar dealing with the Church Fathers' use of Plato were to give an account of recent interpretations of the Dialogues.

[118] *Maier*, pp. 77-78, defends Paul's exegesis here. *Michel* finds Paul's procedure understandable in 10:6-7, if the synagogue understood Deut. 30 as the law and played the passage off against Christian preaching. Bonsirven, *op. cit.*, pp. 306-07, holds that Paul's interpretation does not arise from the text but is due to divine inspiration.

given these words by the Jews, who have used Deuteronomy 30 against Christian preaching (so *Michel*, see note 118), or else Paul is here using the passage to put forward an argument.[119] The Jews have held that it would require an effort to bring the Messiah down from heaven. Israel must repent before the Messianic era can begin.[120] This Jewish idea is incorrect: no effort is needed to bring the Messiah down from heaven, for he has already come and is here in his word. Confronted with the Christians' belief in Jesus as the Messiah, the Jews point to the fact that Jesus is dead, so that it would be necessary to descend to the kingdom of the dead to bring him up,[121] if one believed him to be the Messiah. Not at all, says Paul. No, a man must acknowledge Jesus, who is already here, as the Messiah (*Kyrios*), and believe in one's heart that God raised him from the dead.[122] Thus the two elements that explain the statement about ascending into heaven and descending into the abyss are built upon the double confession to follow, and are aimed at Jewish objections to the Christian preaching about Jesus. Comparison with Philippians 2:5-11 already carried

[119] That Deut. 30:11 f., expanded with Psalm 107:26, existed independently of Paul seems to appear from Git 84a Bar (= Baba Metzia 94a, cf. *Billerbeck*, III, 281), unless it is in these texts a stock expression for the impracticable (IV Esdras 4:8; Jub. 24:31). Philo uses Deut 30:11-14 in *De virtutibus (De paenitentia)*, 183 and has preserved "beyond the sea." In another passage, *Quod omnis probus*, 68, Philo uses only Deut. 30:14. Cf. Werner Bieder, *Die Vorstellung von der Höllenfahrt Jesu Christi* ("Abhandlungen zur Theologie des Alten und Neuen Testaments," Zurich, 1949) pp. 71-75.

[120] Cf. *Billerbeck*, I, 162-65; IV, 860 (notes *d* and *e*), 992, 993 (note *d*), 1006, 1007. Oscar Cullmann in "Le caractère eschatologique du devoir missionnaire et de la conscience apostolique de S. Paul. Étude sur le κατέχον(-ων) de II Thess. 2:6-7," *Revue d'Histoire et de Philosophie Religieuses*, 16 (1936), pp. 210-45, holds that this Jewish idea is to be regarded as the basis for Paul's conception of the preaching of the gospel to the Gentiles; it is the factor which still delays the second coming. This is the thought behind Rom. 10:14 where the necessity of preaching is established (pp. 235-36).

[121] The two verbs, ἀνάγω and κατάγω are used in Wisd. Sol. 16:13 of God: καὶ κατάγεις εἰς πύλας ᾅδου καὶ ἀνάγεις.

[122] Cf. Sirach 51:26c: ἐγγύς ἐστιν εὑρεῖν αὐτήν [i.e., τὴν παιδείαν].

out by *Schlatter*,[123] who does not however make full use of
the comparison, shows a certain resemblance between that text
and Romans 10:4-11. This resemblance does not, however,
seem to lead to any deeper understanding of the two texts.

| Romans | Philippians |
|---|---|
| 10:4: τέλος . . . νόμου Χριστὸς (i.e. at the death on the cross) | 2:8: θανάτου δὲ σταυροῦ |
| 10:6: τοῦτ᾽ ἔστιν Χριστὸν καταγαγεῖν | 2:8: ἐταπείνωσεν ἑαυτὸν . . . |
| 10:7: εἰς τὴν ἄβυσσον τοῦτ᾽ ἔστιν Χριστὸν ἐκ νεκρῶν ἀναγαγεῖν | 2:8: μέχρι θανάτου 2:9: διὸ καὶ ὁ θεὸς αὐτὸν ὑπερύψωσεν |
| 10:9: ἐὰν ὁμολογήσῃς . . . κύριον Ἰησοῦν[124] καὶ πιστεύσῃς . . . ὅτι ὁ θεὸς αὐτὸν ἤγειρεν ἐκ νεκρῶν . . . | 2:11: πᾶσα γλῶσσα ἐξομολογήσηται ὅτι ΚΥΡΙΟΣ ΙΗΣΟΥΣ ΧΡΙΣΤΟΣ 2:10: καταχθονίων |
| 10:12: ὁ γὰρ αὐτὸς κύριος πάντων | 2:11: ΚΥΡΙΟΣ ΙΗΣΟΥΣ ΧΡΙΣΤΟΣ |
| 10:13: . . . τὸ ὄνομα κυρίου | 2:9: τὸ ὄνομα τὸ ὑπὲρ πᾶν ὄνομα |

**10:9-10.** In connection with the indicated parallelism between 10:6 and Philippians 2:5-12, it is interesting that commentators find difficulty in explaining why "confession" is
mentioned in the present passage. To Paul, who according to
Acts 17:18 preached Jesus and the resurrection, the two elements of this creed are not strange. To him the crucifixion and
the resurrection are the heart of the matter. Why is confession
also mentioned here? Does it have something to do with the
quotation in verse 8,[125] or are "faith . . . confession" and "right-

---

123 P. 313 ("die Toten").
124 Even clearer in B sa Cl; H: τὸ ῥῆμα ἐν τῷ στόματί σου ὅτι ΚΥΡΙΟΣ ΙΗΣΟΥΣ.
125 *Dodd*, pp. 165 ff.

eousness . . . life" merely rhetorical parallels (*Althaus*)? Or
should it be interpreted, as it is by Harder[126] on the basis of
"the high value placed on confession in Judaism"? *Pallis* has
suggested that confession here means confession before the
authorities, or something of that kind. This is probably correct.
The parallel passage in Philippians 2 speaks of an eschatological
confession of Christ as *Kyrios* along the lines of the confession
in heaven when the Lamb enters into heaven (Revelation 5).
This eschatological confession, however, presupposes the earthly
confession of Christ as Lord, which may at any moment become
the responsibility of the faithful before the authorities. Paul
at this time was thinking of his forthcoming journey to Jerusalem and the confession he would make before his people and
possibly before the Sanhedrin.

In 10:11 the quotation from 9:33b is repeated with the
addition of $\pi\hat{a}\varsigma$. The words of the quotation apply not only to
the Gentiles, but also to the Jews. $\pi\hat{a}\varsigma$ is further explained in
verse 12 by $o\dot{v}$ . . . $\delta\iota\alpha\sigma\tauo\lambda\acute{\eta}$ (there is no distinction between
Jews and Greeks). According to verses 9 ff., $\kappa\acute{v}\rho\iotao\varsigma\ \pi\acute{a}\nu\tau\omega\nu$ is
Christ, while $\dot{\epsilon}\pi$' $\alpha\dot{v}\tau\hat{\omega}$ in verse 11 (and also in 9:33) applies to
Christ. Earlier, in 3:29, Paul stated that he was the God of
both Jews and Gentiles (*Lagrange*). As scriptural evidence he
cites Joel 2:32 (LXX, 3:5): "Every one who calls upon the
name of the Lord will be saved." [127]

## 10:14-21: God has done everything in order that the Jews may believe and call upon Christ.[128]

It is surprising that commentators are almost unanimous in
agreeing that the aim of chapter 10, including 10:14-21, is to
demonstrate Israel's guilt. It seems natural to them that Paul

[126] G. Harder, *Paulus und das Gebet* (Gütersloh, 1936) p. 107 as quoted
by *Michel*, p. 229, note 1. I have not had access to the volume by Harder.

[127] This text, which in Acts 2:17 ff., 39 is interpreted as applying to the
Jews only, is interpreted here as applying to both Jews and Gentiles.

[128] Cf. *Bardenhewer* on 10:14-21, and *Maier*, p. 87.

should continue the thought of chapter 9—where it was shown that God hardens whomever he wishes—by showing that God deals justly in hardening Israel because Israel is already guilty. But there is nothing so important to an exegete as what the text says or does not say. In this case, of course, Israel's guilt is actually mentioned but is not stressed as a main theme. The most to be found is a description of Israel as "a disobedient and contrary people" in the 10:21 quotation, but Paul is not labeling this as guilt any more than he does Israel's negative attitude in verses 3 and 16.

It would facilitate the understanding of chap. 10 if it were admitted that chapter 9 ends (at 9:29) on more or less the same note as that with which chapter 11 begins: the general obduracy of the people, apart from a chosen remnant. This means, then, that 9:30—10:21 ought to be studied as an independent section which, while a part of the whole—chapters 9-11—must nevertheless be interpreted on its own merits. Only in this way can one link together the three passages in such a way that chapter 11 clearly resumes the thread of 9:29, but, as it were, a little further back—since the intervening passage has explained some pertinent problems: how the unbelief of the Jews has become a reality of the day; what is meant by salvation in Christ; and the fact that God, in spite of the people's crucifixion of the Messiah, has not ceased to call his people through the apostles. Thus this intervening passage is not some incidental parenthesis, but a necessary and basic explanation. Thus, although Paul in chapter 11 obviously returns to the topic he laid aside in 9:29—namely the remnant —he has in fact advanced much further than in chapter 9, so that he is able to give a solution to what in chapter 9 still seemed insoluble.

The concluding quotation in 10:21 reveals the whole sweep of the Israel problem as Paul and the early Christians saw it. At one and the same time the chosen people is (1) the subject of God's invitation to salvation through the apostles whom he has called and who have gone forth to the Jews throughout the earth, and (2) is hardened by God, so that only a remnant of Israel and the elect among the Gentiles come together to form God's new people. The apostolate is a testimony to God's gracious will toward Israel, while at the same time Israel's unbelief expresses God's hardening of their hearts. In a way, chapter 10 makes the problem logically insoluble. The logical contradiction, however, includes the very factors that point the way to a solution. God's hardening implies a redemption purpose toward the Gentiles. The apostolate—and, as we shall see, the remnant—testifies to God's will to save, which is to achieve its purpose after the hardening has fulfilled its function. God hardens in order to save, and he will therefore save the obdurate as well.

The passage introduced by 10:14-15 extends the line of thought begun in verses 3-13—concerning the new way to salvation, the righteousness based on faith—and describes (1) how the news of this salvation is spread abroad and (2) how God has let it be brought to the Jews throughout the earth. But these first two verses only establish the necessity of sending out apostles so that the gospel may be preached, heard, and believed, and so that the invoking of Christ's name may become a reality. But even though these introductory verses deal with prerequisites that apply to Greeks and Jews alike, they are here written, as verses 16 ff. show, with the Jews in mind. The subject of ἐπικαλέσωνται in verse 14 is not, as held by *Weiss* and by *Sanday and Headlam*, taken from the preceding passage, namely those who according to the quotation in verse 13 have achieved salvation by calling upon the name of Christ. Paul is already thinking of those who do not call because they do not believe, etc., anticipating ἀλλ' οὐ πάντες in verse 16. For the moment he makes a fundamental statement of what is needed in order to achieve the goal mentioned in the quotation, namely the invoking of Christ's name for salvation. The subject of ἐπικαλέσωνται and the verbs following it must therefore be taken to be the indefinite pronoun "one,"[129] and the two verses show the necessity of the early Christian apostolate (ἀποσταλῶσιν) if Christ is to be invoked by the Gentiles and Jews. One cannot call without faith, cannot believe in Christ without hearing him, and cannot hear unless an apostle preaches in place of Christ. οὗ cannot be regarded as the adverb of place "where," but must be the genitive of the relative pronoun ὅς, and must here stand for Jesus. When the next sentence sets a preaching apostle in the place of Christ, it must be because the herald who has been sent speaks for Christ. Through him they hear Christ's voice and speech.[130]

**10:15.** The sending out of preachers of the gospel is the primary condition if the Lord is to be called upon for salvation. And this condition has been fulfilled, as the citation of Isaiah 52:7 shows: preachers have been sent out. Paul's exposition of Deuteronomy 30:14 in verse 8, "that is, the word of faith which we preach," is given its scriptural justification in verse 15, as pointed out by *Maier* and *Moe*. Paul gives a very free rendering of Isaiah 52:7 in comparison with the LXX, but possibly he is not using the LXX here. The alteration from singular to plural in εὐαγγελιζόμενος fits the thus designated apostles.

**10:16.** Although the early Christian apostolate to Jews and Gentiles has thus been established, the invoking of Christ has not become general: "They have not all heeded the gospel." The οὐ πάντες here is reminiscent of the οὐ πάντες in 9:6, and shows at once that Paul is now no longer speaking of the

---

[129] Cf. F. Blass and A. Debrunner, *A Greek Grammar of the New Testament and Other Early Christian Literature*, translated and revised from the ninth-tenth German edition incorporating supplementary notes of A. Debrunner by Robert W. Funk (Chicago: The University of Chicago Press, 1961) Sec. 130, p. 72.

[130] Cf. those passages in the Gospels where the emissary represents his Lord: Matt. 10:40; Luke 10:16; in Paul: II Cor. 5:20; Gal. 4:14. In this connection see *Zahn*.

apostolate as a whole. Having considered the necessity of the apostolate in principle and having established that it is being put into practice (by quoting Isaiah 52:7 in verse 15) he now focuses on the apostolate to the Jews. This gentle "not all," which might well be rendered "hardly any of the Jews," is testified to by Isaiah 53:1: "Lord, who has believed what he has heard from us?" Those who are speaking are the apostles, who have been sent out to preach to the Jews. They are addressing Christ who sent them and recounting their troubles. No one has believed the message with which Christ entrusted them. We have a parallel to this apostolic statement in a speech by Peter, the first among the apostles to the Jews, as related in the story of the miraculous draught of fishes, Luke 5:1-11. There Peter says to Jesus (verse 5): "Master, we toiled all night, and took nothing."

10:17 has been greatly neglected by scholars, being regarded as a repetition of verse 14 f. (*Lietzmann* and *Althaus*), or as a connecting parenthetical remark (*Peterson*).[131] The right view is to be found in *Maier*,[132] who holds that the line of reasoning in verse 17 is inspired by Isaiah 53:1, quoted in verse

---

[131] In "Zwei Marginalien im Brief des Paulus an die Römer," *Zeitschrift für die Neutestamentliche Wissenschaft*, 40 (1941), pp. 249-54, Friedrich Müller assumes that 10:13-18 were originally in the following order: vv. 13, 14, 15b (the quotation), 15a, 17, 16, 18. In "Glossen im Römerbrief," *Theologische Literaturzeitung*, 1947, cols. 197-202, Bultmann assumes that 10:17 is a glossator's marginal comment. *Michel* agrees with Bultmann. Cf. also H. W. Wolff, *Jesaja 53 im Urchristentum* (3d ed., rev.; Berlin: Evangelische Verlagsanstalt, 1952), pp. 93-4. H. Pope in "A Possible View of Romans X 13-21," *Journal of Theological Studies*, 4 (1903), pp. 273-79, has tried to tackle 17b exegetically, and let it correspond to v. 19, but neither his article nor W. Spicer Wood's with the same title, *ibid.*, pp. 608-10, seems to solve the problem. *Hoppe*, pp. 124-26, finds a solution to the ἄρα that connects v. 17 with v. 16 (after a reference to Büchsel) in that this ἄρα alludes to a wider sphere of thought (vv. 8-16): "Paul, having reached his goal in v. 16, makes a new beginning in order to point up still further what he has accomplished. The subject presented in broad outlines above (especially vv. 14 f.) is stated compactly in v. 17, whereas the material touched on so briefly in v. 16 is given broader and more forceful treatment in vv. 18-21" (*Hoppe*, p. 126).

[132] Pp. 91-93.

16. The text shows that there are three elements in the aposto-late to the Jews: faith, the message, and the Lord who has sent out apostles. The last element, at least, is certain. Christ has indeed called and sent out apostles to the Jews, but be-tween the message and the lack of faith there might be some-thing that had not been put into effect: Have the Jews really had the message preached to them?

ἀκοή is used here, in the passive sense of "rumor," some-thing that was heard, very close to ἀγγελία and κήρυγμα.[133] Another word in the verse also needs closer definition, ῥῆμα; it is not a "Pauline" word. Apart from this chapter—10:8 (quotation), 9 (B Cl reading), 17 (the present instance), and 18 (quotation)—the word occurs only in II Corinthians (12:4 and 13:1, in the latter case a quotation).[134] If in verse 17 the word is understood in the same sense as in verses 8 and 18, the meaning will be "word," i.e. the gospel. But appearing here next to ἀκοή it is, in spite of ῥήματα in the neighboring verse (18), most natural to take ῥῆμα as referring to the command given by Christ and in accordance with which the message they heard was brought by the apostles.[135] The apostles here are, of course, the original Christian apostles who have seen the risen Lord and have been sent by him to preach the gospel.

**10:18.** Paul here poses the question left open by the quota-tion in verse 16 and his summary of its content in verse 17: Have they heard? And has this taken place throughout the world? Or can it be said that as a whole they have not heard? Paul dis-

---

[133] *Kittel (E)*, I, 221 f.

[134] It is also used in Eph. 5:26; 6:17.

[135] Attention may be drawn to the common expression in the LXX, ἐγένετο ῥῆμα κυρίου (Gen. 15:1; I Sam. 15:10; II Sam. 7:4; I Kgs. 12:24 [v. 24y in Rahlfs' short edition of the LXX]; 17:2, 8; 18:1. Cf. 19:9; 20:28; II Kgs. 20:4; Jer. 1:1), where the word of the Lord is simultaneously a message and a call to deliver that message. *Weiss*, who holds the same opinion as that given here, points to the use of ῥῆμα in the same construction (though with κυρίου for χριστοῦ), διὰ ῥήματος κυρίου in the LXX: Ex. 17:1; Num. 33:2; Deut. 34:5. Cf. also Eero Repo, *Der Begriff RHĒMA im Biblisch-Griechischen*, 2 vols. (Helsinki, 1951, 54) II, 81-3.

misses this with a scriptural proof text, Psalm 19:4: "Their voice has gone out to all the earth, and their words to the ends of the world." This verse from the Psalms describes the preaching of the apostles (the twice-mentioned αὐτῶν) to the Jews in all the earth; their preaching is completed. Apart from *Weiss* and *Maier*, commentators have as a rule avoided taking these words literally. *Zahn* considers it foolish to have Paul interpret words clearly dealing with the worldwide proclamation of God's glory through his created works as a prophecy concerning the spread of Christian preaching. Paul, according to *Zahn*, does not give these words as a scriptural text, still less as scriptural proof of a fact that needs none. Leaving all the sacred words intact, he uses their eloquence to express his own thoughts, or rather as a symbolic description of the way in which, even at the time he wrote, the gospel had spread over a great part of the contemporary civilized world. Now it is true, of course, that these words are not expressly quoted as scriptural proof. But the parallel structure—the question μὴ Ἰσραὴλ οὐκ ἔγνω; in verse 19, followed by the answer in verses 19-21—tends to offset the fact that these words have not been introduced by one of the usual quotation formulas that indicate a direct quotation from Scripture will be following immediately afterward. As already remarked, this distinction between quotations from Scripture and the use of biblical texts to express Paul's own thoughts is arbitrary. It is reasonable only when a passage written by Paul contains vague biblical allusions, and even in such cases one must be wary of denying that Paul has alluded to Scripture. The quoting of texts from Scripture cannot without weighty reasons be reduced to a mere appropriation of biblical expressions as a dress for one's own thoughts.

*Sanday and Headlam* avoid a literal interpretation of the words in another way. They say: "As a matter of fact the Gospel had not been preached everywhere. . . . But all that St. Paul means to imply is that it is universal in its character."[136]

136 P. 299.

*Lagrange,* while rejecting such an interpretation, comes closer to a literal interpretation: he regards the statement as an answer to the question of verse 18. Christianity was spreading everywhere in the Mediterranean countries. Therefore the Jews could not truthfully claim ignorance as an excuse. All these interpretations must be rejected. Paul asks whether the Jews have heard, and he answers his question with a text from Scripture that says that the gospel has reached all Jews throughout the world.

From Paul, talk of this kind cannot cause surprise. As regards the Jews, he believes that the gospel has been preached everywhere in the world. This is not the case for the Gentiles, however, as shown by 15:14-24. Among the Gentiles, work in the East has indeed been completed (from Jerusalem and "as far round as Illyricum," 15:19), and after the journey to Jerusalem Paul is going via Rome to the West in order to begin his work in what is as yet an untouched Gentile region. But the mission to the Jews is already completed. This field, which according to Galatians 2:7-10 had been assigned to the apostle Peter, has, like Paul's mission to the Gentiles, occupied a number of apostles (in the sense of missionaries sent out by Christ; it is uncertain whether any of the twelve "apostles" apart from Peter took part in the work). These apostles have now finished the Jewish mission in the sense that they have penetrated all Jewish regions with the gospel. And the result of their work is discussed in this very passage, Romans 9-11. How could it happen that the chosen people has refused the Gospel and become obdurate?

How is it possible that a small number of apostles could deal with all the Jews within such a short time? This question corresponds exactly to another question put in Romans 15: How can Paul now have finished with the East? It is worth considering this second question first. We know of many churches founded by Paul and his fellow-workers before the letter to the Romans was written. They are, if we count Cyprus and Antioch

(in Syria) as belonging to the Jewish apostolate, the following: Pisidian Antioch, Iconium, Lystra, Derbe, Ephesus
(Colossæ and Laodicea), Troas, Philippi, Thessalonica, Beroea,
Athens, Corinth, and Cenchreæ. There are of course other
churches which, like Colossæ and Laodicea, are the result of
Paul's missionary work in a larger center nearby; and furthermore, other apostles have worked in these regions,[137] and in
other areas never mentioned in Paul's letters (or in Acts),
such as Egypt, which probably counted as part of Peter's apostolate to the Jews. Optimistically reckoned, the number of
Christian churches between Jerusalem and Illyria may be esti-
mated at about twice that of the above-mentioned towns. It is
difficult to estimate the number of Christians in these churches,
but an average of a couple hundred will hardly be too little.
The Christians in these areas are thus to be counted in thousands
rather than in tens of thousands. Nevertheless, Paul asserts
that his work in the East is finished.

Paul's statement here, that the apostles to the Jews have
already finished their work and that the outcome is negative,
must be understood in the same way. It is intended just as
literally as the later passage about the Gentiles in the East
(15:19). This obviously differs from any modern way of
thinking, which might perhaps accept the point that the apostles
went to the large centers and started work there, in the hope of
spreading the gospel to the neighboring districts, but which
would never hold that they had finished at so early a stage. In
the era of liberalism, when Paul was credited with such a
modern way of thinking, he was therefore praised without
cause for a missionary strategy that had never occurred to him.
Paul, of course, is not planning ahead for decades and centuries.
He is not thinking of building up and consolidating by means
of an organization. He was called to be an apostle, and the
Gentiles have become his special charge; his task is to preach

---

[137] Such as the apostles Andronicus and Junias, to whom greetings are
sent in Rom. 16:7.

to all Gentiles as soon as possible because the Lord cannot return and bring this world to an end before the preaching to the Gentiles has been concluded. Therefore it is up to Paul when this preaching will reach its conclusion; then the preaching to the Jews can bear fruit and, as we shall see in connection with chapter 11, the Lord can come.[138]

Church after church is added to the Gentile group, but Paul's aim is to complete the work. He does not hold that the apostles are to preach to every single Gentile, but rather that this preaching is to be representatively completed throughout the world, as has now been done from Jerusalem to Illyria. The churches we know of from his letters, and those others we must add, are thus the beginning of that "full inclusion" of the Gentiles discussed in chapter 11. The West remains, and it is there that he will resume work after the journey to Jerusalem and a visit to Rome.

The churches we know of, with some more added, must therefore warrant the statement that the Gentiles from Jerusalem to Illyria have all heard the gospel. The apostle did not intend that every individual person should hear the gospel and make his decision, but all Gentile peoples were to do so, and by making their decision in Corinth, Ephesus, and Philippi the peoples in question would decide for or against Christ. The gospel has thus been received representatively by the peoples in question, and this is enough to allow the apostle to travel on— to the Gauls, the Spaniards, and the Britons.

Similarly, we must imagine that Israel's rejection of the gospel is a representative action. It does not mean that every single Jew has heard the apostles preach and has decided against the gospel; rather, the people have shown their unbelief representatively. In the fashion of modern individualistic thinking one cannot say that the Jews crucified Jesus, that by shouting "Crucify him!" the Jewish people killed the promised Messiah. But in the opinion of Paul and his contemporaries

[138] Cf. PSM, pp. 36 ff.

this was held to be the fact. The Jews had killed the Messiah, and after his death they had refused to believe the gospel concerning him. And subsequently they treated the apostles sent out by Christ in the same way: they rejected them and persecuted them (I Thessalonians 2:14-16).

There is indeed a "remnant" which has believed, and with the Gentile Christians forms the true Israel. This remnant is at one and the same time the sole possessor of God's promise— in contrast to the people as a whole, who have said no to the Messiah and hardened their hearts against the gospel. This remnant is concrete evidence that God has not altogether cast away his people (11:11 ff.).

This "representative" idea is a Semitic way of thinking, and Paul may have absorbed it either from his Jewish environment or from the Old Testament.

**10:19.** The question raised in this verse must cause surprise. Neither in the basic account of the prerequisites for calling upon the Lord, an account which showed a need for the early Christian apostolate (verses 14-15), nor in the conditions of Jewish obedience to the gospel taken from Isaiah 53:1 is there anything about "understanding." But having once established that the Jews have heard but not believed (verses 16-18) Paul introduces yet another possibility into the zone between hearing and believing: The Jews may have heard, but perhaps they have not understood.

*Zahn* offers another interpretation of the verse when he reads: μὴ Ἰσραὴλ οὐκ ἔγνω πρῶτος; and lets the question, "Has Israel not first (of all peoples) become acquainted with (the gospel)?" provide its own answer: Yes, there is a priority here. For all its ingenuity, this interpretation has to be rejected, as *Kühl* shows.[139] *Kühl* is just as correct when he interprets ἔγνω as referring to an intellectual comprehension, not to a consent

---

[139] *Kühl,* p. 362. πρῶτος presumably designates the Moses quotation as the first of a series (here of two or three).

of the will. This is the right interpretation also as against Bultmann's interpretation of ἔγνω here in 10:19.[140] The question whether Israel has understood is answered in the affirmative, like the parallel question in verse 18. The texts quoted—Deuteronomy 32:21[141] in verse 19, and Isaiah 65:1, 2 in verses 20-21—show that although Israel have understood they have, according to Deuteronomy 32:21, been set aside in favor of an ἔθνος ἀσύνετος. And, according to Isaiah 65:1, God has been made manifest to those who were so little qualified to recognize him that they had not even sought him or asked for him.[142] Isaiah 65:2 shows, furthermore, that it was solely rebelliousness and disobedience which prevented Israel from accepting the grace of God offered them "all day long." Yes, indeed they have understood, says Paul in answer to his own question, but while other peoples, ignorant or unqualified, have accepted God, Israel has understood while remaining unwilling to receive his offer of salvation.

The question μὴ Ἰσραὴλ οὐκ ἔγνω must, like the question in verse 18, be answered in the affirmative; in this case, however, the answer is only given in the form of scriptural texts (in verse 18 there is a μενοῦν γε). ἔγνω cannot, therefore, designate a positive appropriation of the message preached (ἀκοή), in the general sense of "acceptance." Rather, it must be understood as presupposing a personal acceptance of the gospel, and, like ἤκουσαν in verse 18, must denote a universal presupposition which is not already supported by recognition and faith but which must not be lacking if the possibility of faith is to be granted to Israel. In this respect the present text differs from other New Testament texts, which state that hardening affects the very sight and hearing, so that it is no longer possible to understand what is preached.

---

[140] *Kittel (E)*, I, 705. Cf. *Kühl*, p. 362.

[141] For Paul's use of Deut. 32 see p. 119, note 176.

[142] The Gentiles possess this qualification, according to Paul's Areopagus address, Acts 17:27.

Thus Isaiah 6:9-10 is quoted in Matthew 13:14-15 and used also in Matthew 13:13, which is a parallel to Mark 4:12 and Luke 8:10; it is also quoted in Acts 28:26-27 and in John 12:40, although in a form differing from that of the other New Testament texts (τυφλόω and πωρόω and nothing of hearing). An interesting point about this Johannine rendering of Isaiah 6:9-10 is that in several New Testament passages (particularly in Matthew) τυφλός is used of one who is blind in the metaphorical sense, while πωρόω and πώρωσις are used to denote hardening of the spirit. Thus πώρωσις in Romans 11:25. (In Ephesians 4:18 it refers to the Gentiles, in Mark 3:5 to hardness of heart in the bystanders.) Also πωρόω in Romans 11:7. (II Corinthians 3:14, also refers to the Jews, while Mark applies the term to the disciples in 6:52 [a comment by the evangelist] and 8:17 [said by Jesus].) Of special interest in respect to Romans 10 is the fact that this text about hardness of heart comes in John 12—just after verse 38, where Isaiah 53:1 is quoted as being fulfilled in the Jews and their lack of faith is explained by quoting Isaiah 6:9-10 in the special Johannine form.

Corresponding to this text from Scripture, that the senses of the Jews are already sealed to the preaching of the gospel (admittedly said only of the eyes in John 12:40), we find in John 8:43, 47; 10:3, 16, 27; 18:37 that only those that are of God ("my sheep") hear the voice of Jesus. The interpretation of the Parable of the Sower in Matthew 13:18-23 says in verse 19, "When any one hears the word of the kingdom and does not understand it (μὴ συνιέντος)," and conversely in verse 23, "As for what was sown on good soil, this is he who hears the word and understands it."[143] In Mark 7:14 Jesus begins his teaching with the words, "Hear me, all

---

[143] Mark 4:20 (Matt. 13:23) has παραδέχομαι; in Mark 4:15 (Matt. 13:19) something is missing which corresponds to συνιέντος. In the Cairo Fragments of a Damascus Document (CDC 7:18) it is said that the people lacks understanding.

of you, and understand (σύνετε)," and when in verse 17 the disciples wish for a further explanation, he says (verse 18), "Then are you also without understanding (ἀσύνετοι)?" In Mark 8:17-18 Jesus reproaches his disciples with the words, "Do you not yet perceive (νοεῖτε) or understand (συνίετε)? Are your hearts hardened (πεπωρωμένην)? Having eyes do you not see, and having ears do you not hear?" The closing words (verse 18) are a quotation from Jeremiah 5:21.

If we consider the passages that mention seeing and hearing and understanding, together with the hardening that has affected now one function, now all, we find, as with most other concepts in the New Testament, that the statements are ambiguous. In some instances it may be difficult to distinguish between "understanding" and "recognition." That the New Testament writers did not aim at an unequivocal use of these concepts is best seen, perhaps, in Romans 9-11, where Paul, in 11:8, shortly after 10:19, quotes with reference to Israel's obduracy: "God gave them a spirit of stupor, eyes that should not see and ears that should not hear, down to this very day" (Deuteronomy 29:4). There is here an evident contradiction of Romans 10, where it is heavily stressed that the Jews had both heard and understood. Nevertheless, the train of thought is clear enough, for in chapter 10 the purpose was to establish that the message had reached all Jews throughout the world, and that it was brought to them in a comprehensible form (cf. 10:8), while 11:8 and 10:21 explain that it was from within that they were shut off from everything that could break the vicious circle of the self-chosen way to salvation, of disobedience, and of rebellion against God and his Messiah.

In the opinion of *Lagrange,* verse 19 proves that ἀγνοοῦντες in verse 3 referred to a culpable ignorance, but if in this verse we assume an affirmative answer to the question, then there is a wide difference between the Jews' attitude to the preaching of the gospel by the apostles and their attitude to Jesus during his life on earth. Admittedly the final result in both cases will be

the same, namely disobedience, but with a difference: at the
time of the incarnation they were ignorant, while now there is
recognition. The quotations that could be added to the statement in verse 3 point to the conclusion that ἄγνοια is somewhat
typical of their reaction to Jesus' crucifixion and death. This is
not so, however, at the time of the apostles, when the Jews hear
and understand, but retreat into a stubborn disobedience to the
gospel, into obduracy.

The point of the quotation in verse 19 is ἐπ᾽ ἔθνει ἀσυνέτῳ,
and it is to Paul a text of fundamental importance, reap-
pearing in 11:11, in connection with the introduction of the
παραζηλῶσαι, which in turn leads into the decisive discussion
of Paul's missionary strategy in regard to Israel: to win the
Jews for the gospel through ζῆλος.

10:20 concerns the Gentiles, not the Jews (*Lagrange*),
and shows how God allowed himself to be found by the Gentiles in spite of their previous disobedience (Romans 1:18 ff.),
when they walked without God.[144] If the Gentiles could hear,
understand, and receive, then the Jews obviously cannot use
the excuse that they did not understand when they heard.

10:21. The point of the quotation from Isaiah 65:2 is that
Israel has been disobedient and contrary.[145] Therefore it cannot be maintained that Israel has not understood. Not the Jews'
intellects but their hearts were what decided that they would
hear but not receive. According to *Weiss*, the verse is trying
to show that disobedience and contrariness are a permanent feature of Israel's character. If so, then Stephen's speech in Acts 7,
with its attack on the Jews for their conduct right from the
time of Abraham to the speaker's own day, would be a parallel
to this verse. But it is hardly reasonable to regard the quotation as proof of a perennial peculiarity of character in Israel.

[144] Cf. Acts 14:16 and 17:30 on the times of ignorance.
[145] It should be added that Isaiah 65:2 after the phrase "a rebellious
people" continues "who walk in a way that is not good, following their own
devices," which is reminiscent of Rom. 9:31 f. and 10:1 f.

Here in chapter 10, as in chapter 9, Paul is dealing with the present and its circumstances, and the citations of Scripture describe the present situation because they were written not only for the sake of Israel in the past but also for the sake of "us," who live in the age of fulfillment (cf. Romans 4:23-25; I Corinthians 10:11).

*Maier* is right in maintaining that the quotation shows the Jews' circumstances differing from those of the Gentiles. In respect to the Jews it is not simply a question of God's allowing himself to be found, of his becoming manifest to them, but of an untiring activity on his part; he strives with love for his people, even though said people respond to his love with disobedience and contrariness.

This particular verse could be understood as stressing Israel's disobedience in order to show its guilt, though the guilt is not expressly mentioned.[146] This verse, however, does not dwell on the guilt of the Jews, but moves briskly on, through their fall and obduracy, to God's salvation at the last time.

**11:1-36. To the question, "Has God rejected his people?" Paul gives a negative answer, showing (1) that the rejection of Israel is only partial (verses 1-10); (2) that it is only temporary (verses 11-27); (3) that there has been a purpose in all this, deeper and wiser than mankind can understand (verses 28-36).[147]**

**11:1-10. The partial rejection of Israel.**

The apostles travel to the ends of the earth to show that God's hands are stretched out toward Israel, and they are called by God. They, therefore, would seem to be a flagrant contra-

[146] This is the case with Luke 11:49 (which is more topical in expression than the parallel Matt. 23:34) concerning the sending of prophets and apostles to Israel, some of whom the Jews will slay and persecute. Israel's guilt is here stressed in Luke 11:50-51.

[147] So *Sanday and Headlam*, pp. 353 ff., who, however, separate vv. 11-25 from vv. 26-36.

diction to Israel's unbelief, Israel's rejection of the gospel, and Israel's persecution of those who bring that gospel, since Israel's obduracy is likewise God's work. Which of the two components of this contradiction is the truth in regard to God's sentiment and will toward Israel? Are we to regard their unbelief as the true symptom of God's purpose for his chosen people? In reality he has already rejected Israel. Does not the complaint of the patient but weary apostle to the Jews in 10:16, "Lord, who has believed what he has heard from us?" already contain a warning that they must soon abandon the task, and themselves admit that God has rejected Israel? Paul grants all the pessimistic things that can be said of the Jews in their relationship to the gospel, but as early as chapter 10 he was laying the groundwork for a decisive negation of the idea that Israel is to be rejected—by showing that God will not abandon his attempts to save Israel. The despondent but never despairing apostles to the Jews have seen with their own eyes the picture Paul has been painting, yet set out once more to preach Christ, and in so doing they mirror the desire in God's heart to save his erstwhile chosen people through the channels of grace.

11:1. According to *Weiss* and *Lagrange*, οὖν refers back to 9:30—10:21, and this is true insofar as what is stated in chapter 11 presupposes the whole tenor of thought developed in the preceding passage; but it is more natural to let οὖν refer to the particular statement that immediately precedes it, i.e., that Israel has heard and understood but has not received the gospel. In the immediately preceding verse, 10:21, we find God's manifestation of his tireless will to save Israel sharply contrasted with the disobedience and contrariness of the people.[148] As mentioned above, Paul returns in 11:1 to the train of thought found at the end of 9:6-29, especially the idea of the remnant; he returns, however, to that point in such a way

---

148 *Zahn* also links 11:1 with the quotation in 10:21, in that Paul, on the basis of Isaiah 65:2, believes that God also stretches forth his hands to Israel in the present. On that basis he can make the statement in 11:1.

that he is able, by virtue of the intervening passage, 9:30—
10:21, to solve the problem posed without being misunderstood
by his readers.

The question concerns the present generation of Jews. Does
its disobedience to the gospel, the obduracy determined by God,
mean that God has rejected his people? This question might
reasonably be asked by the apostles to the Jews when their labors
proved fruitless (10:16). The same question might also be
asked by the Gentile Christians, who saw the natural olive
branches broken off the good olive tree in order that they themselves might be grafted in (11:19). But Paul only poses the
question in order to make short work of it.[149]

His first answer is a reference to himself. He belongs to
Israel, and yet he is a Christian. As in the case of the remnant,
introduced later, this may be taken as a demonstration from his
own case history: the very existence of Christian Jews is evidence that the Jewish people as a whole cannot have been rejected. This can then be taken in two ways: either Paul regards
himself as a single example,[150] or Paul, in his capacity of
apostle, does not merely belong to Israel, but has a task to perform for his people, as 11:13-14 shows.[151] It is not unlikely
that Paul is giving himself as an example because his personal
disobedience and contrariness toward Christ—as a persecutor of

[149] The sentence οὐκ ἀπώσεται κύριος τὸν λαὸν αὐτοῦ is found three times in
the LXX: I Sam. 12:22; Psalm 93:14; 94:4 (B). Psalm 93:11 (LXX) is
quoted by Paul in I Cor. 3:20.

[150] *Jülicher's* view, that Paul is far too warmhearted a patriot to admit that
10:21 is the last word in the matter, must be rejected. Patriotism in the ordinary secular sense does not occur in the New Testament, and in Rom. 9-11
Paul is engaged in discovering God's plan, not in setting forth his own views.
On the other hand, *Jülicher* (as also *Kühl*, p. 365) is right in pointing out
that to refer solely to his own example would be tactless in addressing a
church of Jewish Christians.

[151] *Gaugler*, II, 161-62, holds that in citing himself as an example Paul
wishes primarily to state that Christ has made him, an Israelite, into an
apostle. If God had wished to save only the Gentiles, or only a few of Israel,
he would hardly have taken the apostle to the Gentiles from Israel. This argument is, however, hardly Pauline because the apostles, including those to the
Gentiles, are all—or at least nearly all—Jews.

the church and the revelation he experienced on the way to Damascus, which made him a Christian and an apostle—make him a kind of promise and an example to Israel as a whole (*Maier*).[152]

Too much consideration should not be given to the expressions used in describing Paul's Israelitic origin (cf. Philippians 3:5; II Corinthians 11:22). This kind of thing could not be done briefly, or without a flourish.

11:2. Here two further arguments are introduced to counteract the suggestion that God has rejected Israel. Instead of the μὴ γένοιτο of verse 1, Paul now changes his tone from a questioning statement to one of denial: οὐκ ἀπώσατο ὁ θεὸς τὸν λαὸν αὐτοῦ and adds: ὃν προέγνω. The fact that God has foreknown his people, i.e., has chosen them, makes it impossible that he should now reject them. προγινώσκειν denotes election and refers to God's earlier choice of Israel to be his people.[153] To this one might object that the original decision is no argument against the rejection of the people now; similarly, *Jülicher* on verse 16 quite logically points out, albeit with a certain lack of respect toward the apostle, that Paul's conclusions are not unassailable. He appears to be referring to Paul's dismissal (in 9:6 ff.) of the idea that one's ancestry gives a

---

[152] Paul used God's call to him, through a revelation of Jesus Christ at Damascus, as an element of his preaching, as appears from the largely uniform versions of the story in Gal. 1:13-17; Acts 9:1-19a; 22:3-16; 26:4-18 (cf. PSM, pp. 11-35). It is obvious that a man who unexpectedly and unwillingly became the servant of God and his Christ would understand what was meant by God's ἐκλογὴ ψάριτος.

[153] Cf. Bultmann's article in *Kittel (E)*, I, 715. προ- in προγινώσκειν does not necessarily mean that the decision was made before the creation. προ- merely means earlier in relationship to something else, here the possible rejection. Similarly, πρωγινώσκω and προορίζω in Rom. 8:28-30 denote that the call and the (still future) glorification, etc., were preceded by election. (Both E. von Dobschütz, "Prädestination," in *Zeitschrift für Theologie und Kirche*, 106 [1934/35], pp. 9-19, and K. L. Schmidt in *Kittel (G)*, V, 457, 11-28, differ.) The same applies to the verb προητοίμασεν in 9:23 where the preparation for glory takes place in the present, προ- in the verb denoting that the glory is as yet in the future, and corresponding stylistically to the preposition in κατηρτισμένα in v. 22.

right to salvation. But Jülicher has misunderstood the apostle. Paul maintains at one and the same time that the Jew has no right to wave his pedigree in God's face and that God, in his sovereign grace, is merciful toward the people whom he graciously chose from the beginning (cf. 11:28-29).[154] Israel's election is in one sense unshaken, but still dependent upon God's sovereign grace. The Jew, therefore, must now receive this grace by faith in Christ and his resurrection (10:9).

The second argument adduced—or rather introduced—in verse 2 is a reference to the word (ὁ χρηματισμός) God addresses to Elijah (verse 4) when the latter complains against Israel (verse 3). This argument presupposes that the "remnant" idea is an assurance for the whole people of Israel: the very existence of such a remnant proves that Israel has a future.[155]

11:3. Paul here gives a free quotation from the LXX, I Kings 19:10, 14. And in verse 4 he quotes 19:18. What was thus written about Elijah—and Paul is perfectly able to distinguish between his own day and that of Elijah, as is evident in verse 5—is of significance to Paul and his contemporaries. But the Elijah quotation in verse 3 merely describes Paul's situation, not his mood. He does not make intercession to God against his people; only his situation is like Elijah's. In terms of the quotation's frame of reference, the majority of the people have followed Ahab in his persecution of Jahwe worship; in Paul's situation they have followed the Jews of Palestine in their rejection of the gospel, so that Paul also is alone and in danger of his life. As we know from his letters,[156] it is almost

[154] In his letters, Paul on several occasions stresses that God is faithful and will finish what he has begun. So Rom. 3:2-3; I Cor. 1:9; 10:13; II Cor. 1:18; I Thess. 5:24; II Thess. 3:3 (of Jesus). Cf. II Tim. 2:13; Heb. 10:23; 11:11; John 1:9. This applies not only to the church but also to Israel.

[155] ἐν Ἠλίᾳ was a current way of quoting. Cf. *Sanday and Headlam,* pp. 310-11; *Billerbeck,* III, 288. Also ἐπὶ τοῦ βάτου, Mark 12:26 (see *Billerbeck,* II, 28; *Sanday and Headlam,* p. 311, differ).

[156] See Excursus 1, "Israel as Persecutor," above, pp. 49-55.

always the Jews who start persecutions in an effort to prevent him from preaching the gospel and to destroy him.

It would seem natural to Paul, at the time he was writing the letter to the Romans, to point to Elijah as the figure in *Heilsgeschichte* who has a task to fulfill toward his unbelieving people. Paul's approaching journey to Jerusalem had points of resemblance to Elijah's return to Israel in order to renew the struggle with a showdown on Mount Carmel. After many years' work among the Gentiles from Antioch to Achaia, Paul was now going up to Jerusalem with the gifts from the Gentile churches for the poor of the church in Jerusalem; and he planned that this presentation from the Gentiles, who had received the promises given to Israel, would rouse the people's jealousy and thus break their obduracy, preparing them to receive the Gospel. Elijah on his way to Mount Carmel and Paul heading for Jerusalem are much alike. Both are risking their lives by going to Palestine, and both aim in God's name to change the destiny of their people by making them believe in God and persuading them to turn away from the error that has made them his enemy.

11:4. καταλείψεις (God's word to Elijah in I Kings 19:18, LXX) is here changed to God's κατέλιπον which agrees with the Masoretic text. Dillmann's explanation[157] of τῇ Βάαλ is that the objectionable *Baal* has been read as *bosheth* and that in the LXX αἰσχύνη has been read for "Baal." The feminine article with the masculine name of the divinity Baal is then a sign of this *Qeré*. Lagrange rightly dismisses the suggestion that Paul is not now using scriptural proof. The seven thousand are a proof that God has not rejected his people.[158] There is

---

[157] C. F. A. Dillmann, "Über Baal mit dem weiblichen Artikel (ἡ βάαλ)" *Monatsberichte der Königlichen Akademie der Wissenschaften zu Berlin* (Berlin, 1881) pp. 601-20.

[158] Some scholars stress the figure "seven thousand" as representing a not inconsiderable part of the people, but Paul presumably uses it because it is given in the text, regarding it as expressing the remnant chosen by God. If figures are desired, and if we disregard the figures in Acts and keep to Paul's

a difference between the mention of the believing Jews in 9:24 and here. In chapter 9 they are mentioned as distinct from the people as a whole, while here they are mentioned as proof that God has not rejected his people. The idea of a remnant occurs in the Old Testament in the prophets, and is there intended to express the realization of salvation in a remnant of the people: while the people as a whole is faced with destruction, God will preserve a remnant who owe their existence to God's election. Various Old Testament writings lay down a number of requirements expected of this remnant. Not so with Paul, as verses 5-6 show. Precisely because of what they owe to God's grace, the remnant of Israel in Paul's day is living proof that God will finally save the whole people, explicitly stated in 11:26.

11:5. In these latter times God has also preserved a remnant of Israel. The God who has chosen Paul (verse 1) has also chosen this remnant, and he will not reject his people. The word λεῖμμα (earlier ὑπόλειμμα, 9:27c; σπέρμα, 9:29b) has here become κατ᾽ ἐκλογὴν χάριτος. As early as 9:11 it was said of God's sovereign choice (between those descendants of the patriarchs who were to be the children of promise): ἵνα ἡ κατ᾽ ἐκλογὴν πρόθεσις τοῦ θεοῦ μένῃ. Chapter 9 (cf. the quotation in verse 27) emphasized that only a remnant, and not physical Israel as a whole, was to inherit the promise. He wanted to make clear, in other words, that the present situation does not abrogate God's promises, since these have always depended upon election through his sovereign grace; the appended quotations showed how God has prophesied that only a remnant of present-day Israel would be saved. But here, in chapter 11, the remnant concept is put forward in preparation for the message that the whole of Israel will eventually be saved; the stress lies on the

and the Gospels' talk of Israel's unbelief and obduracy, there is every reason to reckon with only a few small churches of Jewish Christians. We have said earlier (pp. 94-99 above) that the Gentile Christians must be counted in thousands rather than tens of thousands; here we may say that the Jewish Christians are to be counted in hundreds rather than thousands.

fact that there is at least a remnant which stands as testimony that God's grace toward the chosen people has not ceased.

11:6. But if the remnant has come into being by grace—the basis of all salvation—then it is no longer by works. If it were by works, then grace would no longer be grace (cf. Galatians 2:21: "If justification were through the law, then Christ died to no purpose"). This was the very way by which Israel tried to achieve righteousness (cf. 9:32) and as early as 9:16 Paul established that it "depends not upon man's will or exertion, but upon God's mercy." *Sanday and Headlam* hold that the present passage does not differ from the earlier statements on election. And they add: "God's people are those whom he has chosen; it is not that the Jews are chosen because they are his people."[159] It is true, of course, that the election comes about by grace, but this statement is not entirely correct. Although the Jew can make no claims upon God by virtue of belonging to the chosen people, God has not, for all that, forgotten the people he originally chose for his own. The following would be the best formulation of this: No one, not even the Jew, can make any claim upon God; but God will save all men in Christ, not only the Gentiles, but Israel also. In his sovereign freedom God chooses to save the people he once freely chose. Such are the difficulties of expressing God's sovereign freedom toward his chosen people.[160]

## EXCURSUS 2. THE CONCEPT OF THE REMNANT IN THE OLD AND NEW TESTAMENTS

The remnant as an Old Testament concept has been treated by Herntrich in Th.W. IV, 200-215, and by Werner E. Müller, *Die Vorstellung vom Rest im Alten Testament,* Inaug. Diss. theol. Leipzig, 1939 (and by several of the writers mentioned below who treat the concept in the New Testament). Paul's use of the concept

159 P. 313.

160 The longer reading, found, e.g., in B and regarded as a later development by most commentators, is defended by *Kühl*, pp. 372 f.

has been treated by Schrenk in Th.W. IV, pp. 215-221. It is not mentioned by him that the concept may occur in the Gospels, but this has been suggested by F. Kattenbusch, "Der Quellort der Kirchenidee," Festgabe etc. A. von Harnack (1921) pp. 143-172, and by K. L. Schmidt: "Die Kirche des Urchristentums," Festgabe für Adolf Deissmann, 1927, pp. 258-319. In England, independently of the development in Germany, the concept has been pointed out by B. H. Streeter, The Primitive Church (1929) pp. 47-49, and by T. W. Manson, The Teaching of Jesus (1931) here consulted in a reprint of the second ed. (1955) pp. 175-188, 193, 210, 227 ff., 248 f., 259, 333. The occurrence of the concept in the Gospels is mentioned in passing by several commentators, e.g., G. Gloege, Reich Gottes und Kirche im Neuen Testament, 1929 (Neutest. Forsch. II, 4), pp. 212-217, 241-249; A. Fridrichsen, "Kyrka och sakrament i Nya testamentet," Svensk teologisk kvartalskrift 12 (1936) p. 306; B. Sundkler and A. Fridrichsen, "Contributions à l'étude de la pensée missionaire dans le Nouveau Testament" (1937) p. 16; J. Schniewind, Das Evangelium nach Markus (1937) in Das Neue Testament Deutsch, I, 1, p. 65; M. Meinertz, Theologie des Neuen Testaments, I (1950) p. 72. In Das Volk Gottes (in Skrifter utgitt av Det Norske Videnskaps-Akademi i Oslo, II, 1941, No. 2) pp. 161-62, with notes pp. 310-311, N. A. Dahl has criticized the supposition that such a concept occurs in the Gospels. A more detailed investigation to ascertain whether the concept really occurs in the Gospel tradition has yet to appear.

11:7. Israel still seeks (present tense) for righteousness, but in its own way rather than by obeying Christ, who is the righteousness of God, in faith. Therefore the people have not obtained what they were seeking; only the elect remnant (ἡ ἐκλογή) have obtained it, and the rest have been hardened. Zahn interprets the hardening to mean that God punishes the leaders and teachers of the people, and those of the people who manifest an advance hostility to the truth. This God does by strengthening them in their resistance to Jesus and the testimony of the apostles. Zahn gives a rather vague description because he does not regard Paul's word as referring to Paul's day, but to some future that is future to us as well. It is more reasonable, however, to take Paul's words as an attempt to understand what is at first quite incomprehensible: that the chosen people did not believe the Messiah sent by God, but killed him, and that the people remained firm in this unbelief toward Christ in spite of the apostles' faithful testimony to the Jews throughout the world. Here, as elsewhere, God's election explains a visible state of affairs. Likewise, the hardening of the Jews is Paul's attempt to describe and explain a visible circumstance. Israel has said no to Christ, and then to the apostles. It has resorted to every expedient to rid itself of these inconvenient witnesses. πωρόω occurs in Job 17:7 (LXX) in the passive.[161] In the New Testament the word is used in John 12:40 in a rendering of Isaiah 6:9 f., which does not agree with the LXX,[162] and in Mark 6:52 (in the passive) of the disciples: ἀλλ᾽ ἦν αὐτῶν ἡ καρδία πεπωρωμένη, in what is clearly a parallel to the quotation in John 12:40. Again in Mark 8:17, they (the disciples) have πεπωρωμένην . . . τὴν καρδίαν ὑμῶν, once more in connection with their lack of belief in the miracles of feeding.[163] In addition to John 12:40 and Romans 11:7, it is used in II Corinthians 3:14 of the Jews: ἀλλὰ ἐπωρώθη τὰ νοήματα αὐτῶν. The noun πώρωσις is used in Mark 3:5 concerning the Jews who are present in the synagogue at the healing of a man with a withered arm—in mentioning their hardness of heart. In Romans 11:25 it is used of the Jews in a manner corresponding to the use of the verb in our present passage. And in Ephesians 4:18 it is used of the Gentiles' hardness of heart, corresponding more or less to the

---

[161] E. Hatch and H. Redpath, *A Concordance to the Septuagint,* 2 vols. (Oxford: Clarendon Press, 1897) II, 1246, also cite Prov. 10:20 where A reads πεπωρωμένος, B S πεπυρωμένος.

[162] K. L. Schmidt, "Die Verstockung des Menschen durch Gott," *Theologische Zeitschrift,* I (1945), pp. 1-17 stresses that the rendering of Isaiah 6:9 f. in John 12:40 corresponds best to the intention of the Hebrew text (p. 13).

[163] In Mark 8:18 either Isaiah 5:21 or Ezekiel 12:2 is quoted, but in either case in a free rendering. Is Isaiah 6:9 f. behind it? This has been suggested by by V. Taylor, *The Gospel According to St. Mark* (London: Macmillan, 1952) p. 367.

state of the Gentiles as described in Romans 1:18 ff. Cerfaux has rightly pointed to a common background for Paul, John, and Mark in their use of "hardness of heart," and has suggested that it might be found in a translation of Isaiah 6:9 f., which made use of precisely this expression.[164]

**11:8-10.** Here scriptural proof of Israel's obduracy is given; first Deuteronomy 29:3, in a free rendering.[165] πνεῦμα κατανύξεως comes from Isaiah 29:10.[166] *Sanday and Headlam* compare the text here to Stephen's speech in Acts 7:2-53, especially 7:51, and maintain: "St. Stephen's speech illustrates more in detail the logical assumptions which underlie St. Paul's quotations. The chosen people have from the beginning shown the same obstinate adherence to their own views and a power of resisting the Holy Ghost; and God has throughout punished them for their obstinacy by giving them over to spiritual blindness."[167] While this is an accurate rendering of the main theme of Stephen's speech, it must definitely be denied that Paul holds the same view. Paul believes that in his own day—the time of Jesus and the apostles—the events in the quotation have already been fulfilled, and the people as a whole have become hardened.

**11:9-10.** The second scriptural proof is taken from Psalm 69:22, 23 (68:23, 24 in the LXX). From this Psalm, verse 4 (LXX, 5) is quoted in the farewell discourses in John, where in 15:25 Jesus, speaking of the Jews' hatred of him and his Father, says that this has come to pass in order that the word might be fulfilled that is written in their law: ἐμίσησάν με

---

164 Lucien Cerfaux, " 'L'aveuglement d'esprit' dans l'évangile de saint Marc," *Le Museon,* 59 (1946), pp. 267-79 (reprinted in *Recueil Lucien Cerfaux,* II, 3-15).

165 Deut. 29:17 is used in Acts 8:23 and quoted in Heb. 12:15 where ἐν χολῇ has become ἐνοχλῇ. Deut. 29:19 is used in Rev. 22:18.

166 Isaiah 29:11 may underlie Rev. 5:1. 29:13 (LXX) is quoted in Matt. 15:8-9 and Mark 7:6-7, and less fully in Col. 2:22. 29:14 is quoted in I Cor. 1:19, and v. 16 in Rom. 9:20. Lastly, there may be a connection between vv. 18-19 and Matt. 11:5. On not seeing and hearing see also pp. 99-102.

167 *Sanday and Headlam,* p. 315.

δωρεάν (LXX: οἱ μισοῦντές με δωρεάν). From the same Psalm, verse 9 (LXX, 10) is quoted about Jesus in John 2:17: ὁ ζῆλος τοῦ οἴκου σου καταφάγεταί με (LXX: κατέφαγέν με), and the second hemistich of the same verse is quoted in Romans 15:3: οἱ ὀνειδισμοὶ τῶν ὀνειδιζόντων σε ἐπέπεσαν ἐπ' ἐμέ (the wording of the LXX). There is on the other hand no parallel in Hebrews 11:26, as is erroneously given in Nestle's *Index locorum*. Only the word ὀνειδισμός occurs here. Verse 21 (22) of this psalm is quoted or alluded to in Matthew 27:34, 48: ἔδωκαν αὐτῷ πιεῖν οἶνον μετὰ χολῆς μεμιγμένον. . . . πλήσας τε ὄξους καὶ περιθεὶς καλάμῳ ἐπότιζεν αὐτόν (LXX: καὶ ἔδωκαν εἰς τὸ βρῶμά μου χολὴν καὶ εἰς τὴν δίψαν μου ἐπότισάν με ὄξος). The same text as in Matthew 27:48 is found in Mark 15:36. In Luke 23:36 we have only the word ὄξος; the same applies for John 19:29.[168]

After this verse (Psalm 69:21) follow the two verses quoted in Romans 11:9-10. It is hardly an accident that verse 21 is used of the death of Jesus on the cross and verses 22-23 of the obduracy of the Jews. Presumably what we encounter here is a common early Christian interpretation of this "Christ psalm." Because the Jews have crucified the Lord Christ, punishment shall therefore overtake them. One may hazard the guess that this was a common early Christian interpretation; but it is not Paul's interpretation.[169] The scriptural citation is used as proof that the remainder were hardened—thus, something which has already come true, and which, as a temporary condition (as what follows will show), is not the divine reckoning which one expects in the confrontation of God with the people who are perpetually disobedient. As with the example of Elijah, so the application of this quotation also illustrates the difference

[168] Psalm 69:24 has influenced Rev. 16:1, and 69:28 (especially "the Book of Life") underlies a number of other passages in Rev. (3:5; 13:8; 17:8; 20:12, 15; 21:27).

[169] There may possibly be traces of this early Christian view in I Thess. 2:15-16. Apart from Paul, it can be found in passages such as those cited above, p. 65.

between the attitude of Paul and the views of other early Christians.

According to *Zahn's* reading of Psalm 69:22-23, Romans 11:8 describes the obduracy of the people, but 11:9-10 recounts the future external judgment upon the temple and city (already prophesied by Jesus) and the later fate of the people in continual exile. *Sanday and Headlam*,[170] we should add, draw attention to the fact that Lipsius, who is not normally fond of interpolation theories, suggests that verses 9-10 are a marginal gloss added by a reader after the destruction of Jerusalem. This supposition indirectly supports *Zahn's* interpretation, but it cannot be justified. Paul is thinking, as rightly assumed by *Kühl* and *Lagrange*, of the obduracy of the Jewish people in his own day. From what has been stated above, it can be assumed that others within the period of early Christianity interpreted the Psalm passage in the way suggested by *Zahn* and by *Sanday and Headlam*.

## 11:11-27. The rejection of Israel is only temporary.

11:11. The question put in 11:11 arises naturally from the preceding account, by which I mean not merely chapter 11, but all the material covered thus far. Only the chosen remnant receives the gospel; the people as a whole refuse it, are hardened, and persecute the apostles. Can these two facts be regarded as the final, unalterable state of things?

The subject of ἔπταισαν is, as *Weiss* rightly remarks, οἱ λοιποί from verse 7, i.e., Israel, with the exception of ἡ ἐκλογή. What does πταίω mean? *Bauer-Arndt-Gingrich* render this passage, "They did not stumble so as to fall into ruin, did they?" and explain further, "the 'stumbling' means *to make a mistake, go astray, sin*."[171] Here ἔπταισαν probably refers back to προσέκοψαν τῷ λίθῳ τοῦ προσκόμματος (9:32) and alludes to

170 P. 316.

171 P. 734. The original German reads, "Sie sind doch nicht angestossen, um zum Fall zu kommen?" and, "Das 'Anstossen' ist *fehlen, irren, sündigen*."

the Jews' rejection of Jesus. πίπτω in the next sentence is rendered by Bauer-Arndt-Gingrich, "fall from a state of grace," and this second verb then denotes their present obduracy.[172] This "stumbling" cannot be the goal the Jews aspire to. Their goal must be rather, as what follows would indicate, something intended by God.[173] When the Jews rejected Jesus, their Messiah, was it God's purpose that they should never rise again after their fall? To this Paul answers in the negative. God turned their stumbling to good—first for the Gentiles, and then for themselves. The question Paul answers here is presumably expressing a point of view that existed in Paul's day. It was assumed that the Jews as a whole had stumbled, the divine purpose being that they should fall.[174] If one compares this question with Paul's subsequent warnings to the Gentile Christians (verse 17 and more especially verse 19) this view was obviously found among Gentile Christians. They assumed, in fact, that the present obduracy was God's final judgment upon Israel, and that salvation was now open only to the Gentiles. But Paul is able to show that the salvation of the Gentiles and the salvation of Israel are not two distinct and mutually exclusive quantities. On the contrary, when Israel stumbled the salva-

---

[172] *Ibid.*, p. 665. The original German is, "aus dem Stand der Gnade fallen." πταίω is generally used in the LXX in the sense "be defeated, fall." πταίω in the New Testament, except in the present instance, always means "to sin." πίπτω is used in the LXX in many passages, but the significance assumed by Bauer-Arndt-Gingrich in Rom. 11:11 can only be regarded as correct in a few instances. *Michel* mentions Isa. 24:20, Psa. Sol. 3:13 (3:10 in Rahlfs' edition). Rom. 11:11 as interpreted by *Bauer-Arndt-Gingrich* is unique in the New Testament. *Michel* cites Heb. 4:11 as a passage in which πίπτω occurs as a metaphorical expression for the final destruction.

[173] *Sanday and Headlam,* also *Lagrange,* dismiss the idea that ἵνα denotes the divine purpose. The difference in interpretation is hardly great, whether one significance or the other is chosen, for *Sanday and Headlam*, p. 321, read μὴ γένοιτο as follows, "St. Paul indignantly denies that the final fall of Israel was the contemplated result of their transgression." There is agreement, therefore, on the question: whether Israel's fall is final or not; most commentators, however, interpret the question: whether or not the fall that follows Israel's stumbling is God's purpose, i.e., whether the fall is their final fate.

[174] Cf. Psalm 19:9 (LXX), αὐτοὶ συνεποδίσθησαν καὶ ἔπεσαν, ἡμεῖς δὲ ἀνέστημεν καὶ ἀνωρθώθημεν.

tion of the Gentiles became God's first intention, and as soon as this intention had been achieved it was in its turn to affect Israel, as a means of influencing the hardened Jewish people so that salvation could also be brought to them. God has decided to use Israel's disobedience to the Messiah as an occasion to bring salvation to the Gentiles—and also, as an end-product, to Israel.[175] This is already implied by the answer given in verse 11, "Through their trespass salvation has come to the Gentiles, so as to make Israel jealous." παράπτωμα, therefore, must refer back to ἔπταισαν, since Paul does not deny this, although he does deny that God thereby intended to let Israel fall from grace forever. παράπτωμα seems to be used in the LXX mainly in a moral sense, for "errors." In the New Testament the word seems more generally used in the same sense, but in Romans 5:15, 17, 18, 20 it is used of Adam's transgression, and here—as in 11:11, 12 where it is applied to Israel's stumbling—we find it is not used with any moral significance, but in reference to an event in *Heilsgeschichte*. Just as Adam's disobedience in the Garden of Eden can be described as τὸ παράπτωμα in chapter 5, so Israel's rejection of Jesus is described in 11:11 as τὸ παράπτωμα. There is, of course, one big difference: the fall of Adam instituted Adamic mankind, while Israel's obduracy is a mere circumstance in the total work of Christ, which has instituted the new mankind, and Israel, despite its obduracy, will one day belong to it. Possibly, however, the use of παράπτωμα is dictated here by the view that Paul rejects. To some of the Gentile Christians, Israel's stumbling would seem an event in *Heilsgeschichte* of the same decisive nature as the fall of Adam.

If the words μὴ ἔπταισαν thus correspond to the clause, "through their trespass salvation has come to the Gentiles," then the divine purpose suggested in ἵνα πέσωσιν, which has

[175] *Althaus* also finds a reference to the idea that Israel's unbelief caused the crucifixion of Jesus, and thus brought about his atonement for the whole world.

been denied, corresponds here to the true divine aim: εἰς τὸ παραζηλῶσαι αὐτούς. παραζηλῶσαι was introduced aready at 10:19 as the quotation from Deuteronomy 32:21; there the scriptural citation was used to prove that Israel had understood the apostles' preaching perfectly well.[176] God's purpose is to make them jealous of a "foolish nation," the Gentiles. This text was obviously of great importance to Paul, since it reappears here with the stress not on the "foolish nation," but on the aim of provoking Israel to jealousy. The succeeding verses will show that what has thus been provided is the practical missionary method to be employed toward Israel.[177] While there are Gentile Christians who hold that Israel's fall is the end of Israel, Paul wants to show that Israel's central position in the *Heilsgeschichte* will become clear precisely in the "last times." Just as Israel's "no" leads to salvation, so will its "yes" be a decisive turning-point later on. Paul's remarks are thus addressed to his own age, as an attack on an erroneous conception among Gentile Christians, and his explanations of ζῆλος are also highly current for his own time.

11:12. πλήρωμα does not, as *Sanday and Headlam, Kühl, Lagrange,* and *Bardenhewer* suppose, refer to "the full number" of Israel, but denotes, in a usage entirely parallel to τὸ πλήρωμα τῶν ἐθνῶν,[178] the conclusion of the Jewish mission, which is thus brought about so that Israel, and no longer merely "the remnant," hears and receives the gospel. It is hardly correct

[176] Moses' song in Deut. 32:1 ff. is used several times in Paul's letters: v. 5 in Phil. 2:15; v. 17 in I Cor. 10:20; v. 21 in Rom. 10:19; 11:11, and in I Cor. 10:22 (another detail from the same verse); v. 35 in Rom. 12:19; v. 43 in Rom. 15:10. It is natural that this bitter attack on Israel—expressed by Moses and a figure of Old Testament redemptive history—should have attracted Paul's attention and that he should have perceived that the judgment is finally averted. Paul was not able to accept the rather obvious implication, viz., that the judgment (which Israel had so well deserved) might be transferred to the enemies of the Jews.

[177] Cf. the remark by von Dobschütz in *Zeitschrift für Systematische Theologie,* 10 (1933) p. 268, note 2.

[178] See pp. 132 ff.

with *Weiss* to apply αὐτῶν solely to the Jews mentioned in verse 11, to whom Jesus had become an occasion for stumbling. The distinction between these and the people as a whole is so slight that Paul can switch directly from one sense to the other. Israel's stumbling proved to be, by God's will, salvation for the Gentiles. Since the Jews did not wish to receive the gospel, this proved to be riches for the world ("the world" here refers to the Gentiles and hence is completely identical with the following ἐθνῶν). Israel's loss through its stumbling became the riches of the Gentiles. Nothing new is stated in this sentence, but by the change from παράπτωμα to ἥττημα, the coming contrast to τὸ πλήρωμα is prepared for. If this is so, if their downfall has brought about so much, how much more will their fullness turn to riches for the world and the Gentiles. τὸ πλήρωμα, therefore, denotes Israel's salvation as opposed to the election of the remnant and the obduracy of the rest. It is of course a truism that Israel's salvation will be of immeasurable importance to the rest of the Gentile world, so that Paul would not be saying anything new in this if the circumstances in which these words were uttered were not so entirely contrary to customary Jewish ways of thinking. As it regards the Gentile Christians, the remark is intended to make plain the importance of the conversion of the Jews, since to many of them this appeared improbable or insignificant.

If we assume, as do some commentators, both that the ἥττημα of the Jews alludes to the fact that in every city they have refused to receive the gospel, and that the remark is thus current and practical as regards Israel's fall at the present day, then it is natural to take what follows as also current and practical. The ζῆλος, then, which Paul is to stir up, and that fullness of the Gentiles which is to lead Israel to salvation, are also to be interpreted as something current and practical. In this passage we get a glimpse of Paul's thoughts as he collects the gift to Jerusalem and gradually realizes that this journey with the collection may turn into a manifestation, a promulgation of the fullness of the Gentiles, something that will impress not only Christians but the Jews in Jerusalem as well. Both in Romans and in Acts we see that the journey to Jerusalem concerns not merely the Jerusalem church but the non-believing Jews of that place as well. Romans 15:31 speaks of the unbelievers in Judea as well as of the saints in Jerusalem, and in Acts 21:11 it is said of Paul that the Jews shall deliver him into the hands of the Gentiles (cf. Matthew 20:19, of Jesus; cf. Acts 21:20 [omit: τῶν πεπιστευκότων[179]]). Paul goes up to Jerusalem fully expecting to effect the great turning point in the life of his people by bringing with him a representation of the fullness of the Gentiles.

**11:13 f.** In *Zahn's* opinion, ἐφ᾽ ὅσον shows that preaching to the Gentiles is a special aspect of Paul's apostolate, which like that of the other apostles is aimed at all mankind and therefore does not exclude efforts aimed directly at Israel. This interpretation, which presupposes that Paul is not solely a missionary to the Gentiles, is possible. Another possibility is to regard Paul as a missionary to the Gentiles who is here explaining that his mission to the Gentiles is an important task because of its significance for Israel. The presupposition, then, is that Israel in its obduracy will not obey the gospel, but that God can reach the Jews with his salvation by another way, i.e., via the Gentiles—through the ζῆλος which their acceptance of the gospel produces among the Jews. But even in this case there is no need to commit oneself to the expression "apostle to the Gentiles," as though it meant that Paul would never dream of approaching the Jews. But while Peter and the other apostles continue to appeal to Israel in spite of its obduracy, Paul has been given the task of preaching the gospel to the Gentiles. And this task, in relation to achieving the salvation of the Jews, is not simply a circuitous method, but the most direct, foretold

[179] Cf. PSM, pp. 238-42.

by God and designed to bring the Jews out of their unbelief and through jealousy to salvation.

When we come to ἐθνῶν ἀπόστολος, the exact significance of the expression must be weighed. Is it a title belonging to Paul alone? Or is it a common designation of those apostles called by Christ to preach to the Gentiles? Analogies from all the other passages in which Paul speaks of his apostolate and his being sent to the Gentiles (Romans 15:15 ff.; I Corinthians 9:15 ff.; Galatians 2:7-9; Colossians 1:24 f.; cf. Ephesians 3:2-11) suggests that Paul occupies a special position, and that to him the role of preaching to the Gentiles has been entrusted.

What is here distinctive is that although Romans 9-11 otherwise deals with peoples and parts of peoples and not with individuals, Paul here introduces his own person, because his call to the apostolate gives him a unique significance for recent events. The preaching of the gospel to the Gentiles, which in Matthew 24:14 is the last event before the coming of the Antichrist, is here regarded as leading not merely to the fullness of the Gentiles but also to the salvation of the whole of Israel. The tasks just completed by Paul, and those which he is about to begin at the time of writing this letter, form the basis for what he writes. He has now completed the mission to the Gentiles in the East (Romans 15:19-24), and intends upon completion of his task in Jerusalem to proceed to the West via Rome (Romans 15:25-32). The collection, which he together with representatives of the Gentile churches is about to take to Jerusalem, is to be a demonstration of the belief of the Gentiles, who have accepted what was promised to Israel before it was accepted by the unbelieving Jews in Jerusalem.

With δοξάζω Paul utters a hymn of praise for his office of apostle (τὴν διακονίαν μου), but adds a clause that expresses the premise of this hymn of praise, "in order to make my fellow Jews jealous, and thus save some of them." The reason why Paul has this at heart is, as expressed in verses 12 and 15, that he believes Israel's salvation to be the supreme event within

*Heilsgeschichte.* He has changed the sequence of events that prevailed in the minds of the earliest disciples—first the preaching of the gospel to Israel, and then to the Gentiles—to the sequence we have learned to know in the preceding pages: the gospel was first to be preached to Israel, but because of Israel's unbelief the Gentiles are now to hear it, and when they have received it Israel will also be saved; but in spite of this, Paul is nevertheless convinced that Israel is still the chief goal of God's will to salvation.

*Survey of the Idea of Mission Within Earliest Christianity*

|  | Jews | Gentiles | Jews |
|---|---|---|---|
| *Jewish Christianity* | YES | YES |  |
| *Paul* | NO | YES | YES |
| *The Post-apostolic Church* | NO | YES |  |

The fact that the Gentiles receive the salvation promised to Israel rouses the jealousy of the Jews, and this brings about salvation. When it is stated that Paul will thus save $\tau\iota\nu\grave{\alpha}\varsigma$ $\grave{\epsilon}\xi$ $\alpha\mathring{\upsilon}\tau\hat{\omega}\nu$, *Weiss* and *Kühl*, also *Maier*,[180] assume a certain humility on the part of Paul, who expects the salvation of all Israel through God's mighty intervention. There is, however, no question of apostolic humility here, any more than there is a distinction between what Paul can do himself and what God will thereafter do. One must not, however, forget the way in which $\tau\iota\nu\acute{\epsilon}\varsigma$ is used in connection with Israel's unbelief. Thus in verse 17 we have $\epsilon\mathring{\iota}$ $\delta\acute{\epsilon}$ $\tau\iota\nu\epsilon\varsigma$ $\tau\hat{\omega}\nu$ $\kappa\lambda\alpha\delta\hat{\omega}\nu$ $\grave{\epsilon}\xi\epsilon\kappa\lambda\acute{\alpha}\sigma\theta\eta\sigma\alpha\nu$, and as early as 3:3 we find $\epsilon\mathring{\iota}$ $\mathring{\eta}\pi\acute{\iota}\sigma\tau\eta\sigma\acute{\alpha}\nu$ $\tau\iota\nu\epsilon\varsigma$.[181] In these passages there can be no doubt that Paul is thinking that Israel as a whole has been unbelieving, and that most of the branches have been

---

[180] *Maier*, p. 126, note 94.

[181] Cf. the use of $\sigma\acute{\omega}\zeta\omega$ in the future in I Cor. 7:16, $\tau\grave{o}\nu$ $\mathring{\alpha}\nu\delta\rho\alpha$ $(\tau\grave{\eta}\nu$ $\gamma\upsilon\nu\alpha\hat{\iota}\kappa\alpha)$ $\sigma\acute{\omega}\sigma\epsilon\iota\varsigma$; and 9:22, $\mathring{\iota}\nu\alpha$ $\pi\acute{\alpha}\nu\tau\omega\varsigma$ $\tau\iota\nu\grave{\alpha}\varsigma$ $\sigma\acute{\omega}\sigma\omega$ where there is also a $\tau\iota\nu\acute{\alpha}\varsigma$, more often read as $\pi\acute{\alpha}\nu\tau\alpha\varsigma$. If this is Pauline humility, it does not concern a small number, but rather a large number modestly viewed as $\tau\iota\nu\acute{\alpha}\varsigma$, an indefinite number.

broken off the good olive tree. It is reminiscent of the οὐ πάντες used in 9:6 and 10:16 of the Jews. It is this careful, almost covert way of speaking of Israel's unbelief and stumbling which explains the use of τινές here, expressing an indefinite number, which the context must define further. As Paul throughout the passage speaks carefully of Israel's unbelief and makes it a matter of τινές and of οὐ πάντες, so τινὰς ἐξ αὐτῶν here must refer to no inconsiderable number. For it is not simply a contrast between the present time, when a very small number of Jews—in contrast to the many—attain salvation, and a time to come when God will intervene to save all Israel. In reality three periods are in question: first, that already described, in which Israel, apart from the remnant, was unbelieving, while the Gentiles received the gospel: next, the period now beginning, when the great results of the mission among the Gentiles begin to make an impression on Israel, so that the tide turns, and an indefinite but not inconsiderable number are won for Christ; and lastly, the decisive and final period, when God intervenes and saves the whole of Israel. Paul sees no decisive difference between this second period with its work of the apostle and its first fruits based on the great success of the Gentile mission, and the approaching period with its salvation of all Israel. Admittedly the latter belongs to the future, but the apostle does not feel himself to be separated from this future as something he cannot take part in and prepare for, even though he himself will not experience it since his task is to be done when the fullness of the Gentiles has been achieved.[182] It is therefore his hope, and a necessary condition for really being able to magnify his office as the apostle to the Gentiles, that the jealousy produced among the Jews by his great results among the Gentiles may lead to that change in the destiny of his people that accords with God's saving will. This final change (11:25) is not an entirely new phase in the *Heilsgeschichte,* but it makes use of that jealousy

---

182 Cf. O. Cullmann's exposition of II Thess. 2:6-7, *op. cit.,* pp. 210-245, and PSM, pp. 36-42.

in the Jews which even now (the apostle feels) is the decisive means for breaking down Israel's present obduracy and for changing the destiny of the people.

The comments made by *Sanday and Headlam* and by *Kühl*— that this verse depicts the Roman church as consisting mainly of Gentile Christians—are not satisfactory. Such individual passages are not needed as proof, but they are useful for confirming what we already know. Both Paul's letters and the picture given of the Pauline churches in Acts show that these churches consist of Gentile Christians.[183] There is no reason to assume, as was formerly done, that the Pauline churches were mixed churches. T. W. Manson's hypothesis concerning the letter to the Romans as a review of fundamentals at the end of the conflicts during the third journey[184] gives rise to an excellent explanation for the fact that Paul here turns to Gentile Christians. This remark is directed to the Gentile Christians in general. In the letter to the Romans, which is a stock-taking intended for other churches than that in Rome, Paul addresses various groups to which he has had the opportunity to speak during the conflicts, and—following my modification of Manson's hypothesis[185]—turns to the Jewish Christians in Jerusalem, and to the Jews. The letter to Rome is both a settling of accounts within the church and an appeal to the Jews.

Finally, it can be said that the chief problem in verse 14 is παραζηλώσω, i.e., the connection Paul has presumed between this jealousy and Israel's salvation. It is obvious that Israel cannot feel jealous of the Gentiles as long as they do not believe that the latter can attain salvation. But as soon as the Jews can see and understand that the Gentiles are going to be given what was promised to Israel the possibility is present that they may become jealous because the promise given to Israel is being received by the "foolish nation" (10:19), and not by themselves.

---

[183] Cf. PSM, pp. 200-09.
[184] See pp. 5-8 above.
[185] See pp. 7-8 above.

11:15. The significance of this result of the Gentile mission is due to the fact that the πρόσλημψις of the Jews will be
of paramount importance. The mention of this, and of the salvation of τινάς in the same breath, shows that the two things
should not be separated, as they are by *Kühl*; rather, the latter
is at all events a prophecy of the former, and presumably the
means of which God will avail himself in his intervention in
order to achieve the salvation of the whole people.

If the ἀποβολή of the Jews (i.e., the casting-away by God
[*Bauer-Arndt-Gingrich*], by which must be meant the hardening God has inflicted on Israel) has brought about the rec-
onciling of the world (i.e., the preaching of the gospel to the
Gentiles; Paul also describes his apostolate as a ministry of rec-
onciliation in II Corinthians 5:18-21) then God's acceptance
of the Jews will mean life from the dead.[186] Both in the writings
of Paul and elsewhere in the New Testament we find life and
death as contrasts, but no close parallel to this expression. The
closest is John 5:24, μεταβέβηκεν ἐκ τοῦ θανάτου εἰς τὴν
ζωήν.[187] The expression has been interpreted as referring to that
life in the aeon to come which begins with the awakening from
death; this interpretation is favored by *Weiss*, who stresses that
Paul does not say ἀνάστασις ἐκ νεκρῶν, because the apostle's gaze
has already traveled beyond this event to its blessed consequence. *Sanday and Headlam* consider another possibility, that
the expression denotes the spread of the gospel and a powerful
spiritual awakening. This is also the view of *Bardenhewer*, who
speaks of "a powerful upswing of Christian faith and Christian living across the whole face of the earth." (*Zahn* comments somewhat similarly.) But this interpretation is subject
to an objection: that one cannot imagine such an increase in
the spread of the gospel after the Gentiles have already received

[186] Cf. the gloss on Sirach 10:20 in Apocrypha, Revised Standard Version
(or see Rahlfs' edition of the LXX).

[187] John 6:33, 51 speak of life unto the world, and Acts 11:18 reads, ἄρα
καὶ τοῖς ἔθνεσιν ὁ θεὸς τὴν μετάνοιαν εἰς ζωὴν ἔδωκεν.

it and the Jews are also being saved. *Lietzmann* is right in saying that a non-eschatological interpretation of the expression
would not call for this increase.[188] *Schlatter* develops the interpretation put forward by *Weiss* by letting the expression denote
the first resurrection. It cannot be the general resurrection, since
"life from the dead" presupposes that there are still some dead
—apart from those who attain life—and that death has not yet
been completely abolished. Although one can hardly force such
a precise understanding upon the expression, it is clear that
its meaning is to be sought among the last events before or
during the Second Coming.

**11:16.** Paul goes on to render such a πρόσλημψις probable.
It is not beyond all probability. If the first fruit be holy, the
lump is also holy,[189] and if the root be holy, so are the branches.
The latter image prepares for the succeeding metaphor of the
good olive tree, and the natural and the wild branches. By the
root Paul means the patriarchs, especially Abraham (cf. Romans
4),[190] and the same applies to the first fruit. It may be pointed
out that in 9:1 f. Paul did actually describe Israel's advantages
in early times. On the other hand there is here no thought of
the remnant as proof of the salvation of all Israel (*Lietzmann*).
In the metaphor the remnant is of course not the root, but those
branches of the true olive tree which have not been broken off,
and among which the wild branches are grafted.

**11:17.** In his usual reticent manner Paul states that τινὲς
τῶν κλάδων[191] have been broken off, while the Gentiles, by
becoming Christians, have been grafted in like wild branches
among the natural branches, and now partake of the fat root

[188] I no longer wish to uphold the interpretation put forward in PSM, pp.
304-05.
[189] Cf. Numbers 15:18-21. See *Billerbeck*, III, 290 and IV, 2, 665-68.
[190] For the plant of righteousness, whose root is Abraham, see *Billerbeck*,
III, 290.
[191] Cf. pp. 123-24 above.

of the true olive tree.[192] The image of the olive tree shows, as is pointed out by *Sanday and Headlam, Lietzmann,* and *Nygren,* that God's people is one and the same throughout the ages.[193] Branches may be broken off and new branches grafted onto the trunk, but the tree remains to draw up sap from its holy root. The new Israel of the church is thus a continuation of the original Israel. *Zahn* is right in saying that Paul is not expressing something agriculturally practicable, but something miraculous; he compares it with John the Baptist's words about raising up children to Abraham from the stones (Matthew 3:9).

## EXCURSUS 3. THE TRUE OLIVE TREE AND THE WILD OLIVE TREE

In "The Olive-Tree and the Wild-Olive," [194] W. M. Ramsay protests against the assumption that Paul was ignorant of methods used in cultivating olives. He points to a remark by Theobald Fischer that in Palestine an olive tree that has ceased to bear is still regenerated by grafting in one of the wild root-suckers, so that the sap of the tree improves it, and the tree once more bears fruit.[195] It is this method Paul is using metaphorically in Romans 11:17, 24. Ramsay also points to Columella, *Res Rustica* V, 9, 16 (ed. E. S. Forster and E. H. Heffner, vol. II [Loeb]) p. 84, 4 from the bottom to p. 86, 5 (cf. Palladius, *Opus Agriculturae* XI, 8, 3 [ed. J. C.

---

[192] For the fatness of the olive tree see Judges 9:9, and Test. Levi 8. Compare συγκοινωνός of the Gentiles with Eph. 3:6. Philo's words about the proselyte in *De Exsecrationibus* 152, reported by *Billerbeck,* III, 291, and the quotation from rabbinical writings in *Billerbeck,* III, 292, show how grafting and the grafted wild branch have been used by others as a metaphor for proselytes.

[193] Cf. Rom. 4:12 and Gal. 3:6 ff.

[194] *The Expositor,* 6th Series, XI (1905), pp. 16-34, 152-60.

[195] T. Fischer, *Der Ölbaum* ("Petermanns Mitteilungen," Ergänzungsheft 147, 1904) p. 9. This information probably derives from G. B. Winer, *Biblisches Realwörterbuch zum Handgebrauch für Studierende, Kandidaten, Gymnasiallehrer und Prediger,* 3rd ed. (Leipzig, 1847) II, 171, note 6, or from the source of this notice, according to *Billerbeck,* III, 291, a mid-eighteenth century traveler, Stephan Schulz (quoted by Winer in *Schulz Leitung,* V, 88), and is hardly of more value than Linder's or Dalman's statements, reported below.

Schmidt, Leipzig, 1898, "Bibliotheca Teubneriana," p. 216, 9-15],
and IV, 8, 2 [p. 121, 15 f.]), and to Palladius, *Opus Agriculturae*
XIV, 53 (p. 264).[196] These classical texts do not seem completely
clear to me, because Columella (on whom Palladius is dependent)
does not state how the grafting-in of a wild olive branch will make
the original tree fertile. There is a later account by S. Linder,[197] of
a method used on olive trees in Greece. When a tree is old, and
can bear fruit only a few years more, one of its roots is laid bare,
and a shoot, often from a wild olive, is placed in an incision in the
root. This shoot soon grows into a sturdy sapling, and begins to
spread into a crown. The wild branches on the new trunk are then
lopped off, and cultivated twigs are grafted. From these a crown
develops, which in a few years begins to bear fruit, while the old
olive tree is felled. This description is used by F. J. Bruijel,[198] to
establish that Paul in Romans 11 is recounting something which
really takes place, and which is therefore not contrary to nature.
G. A. Dalman[199] relates a report from the northernmost part of
Palestine that in Lebanon a wild tree was sometimes grafted onto a
cultivated tree to give fresh strength to the latter. But the wild
branch that grew from this must then in turn be cultivated. And
Dalman mentions Linder's report of a similar method in Greece,
but adds that the idea of grafting a wild branch onto a cultivated
tree struck his Arab friends as both ludicrous and incredible. In
the same connection Dalman dismisses the idea that this present-
day information provides the explanation of the grafting of wild
branches mentioned by Paul in Romans 11, because according to
this the grafted wild branch must first be cultivated, while in Paul's
account the sap of the cultivated tree performs this function.[200] At
this point it would seem to me that Dalman has reached the end
of his rope in this discussion. Paul describes God's dealings in the
*Heilsgeschichte* by means of a metaphor as strange as the reality it
represents. It may be added that the metaphor and the reality be-

[196] It must be added that these references are extremely vague. In the case
of Palladius only the author's name is given, together with the information
that he speaks in verse, from which Ramsay presumably alludes to *Liber XIV*.

[197] "Das Pfropfen mit wilden Ölzweigen (Rom. 11:17)," *Palästinajahrbuch*,
26 (1930), pp. 40-43.

[198] "De Olijfboom," *Gereformeerd Theologisch Tijdschrift*, 35 (1934),
pp. 273-81.

[199] *Arbeit und Sitte in Palästina*, 6 Vols. (Gütersloh, 1928-39) IV, 184-85.

[200] Cf. Fischer, *op. cit.*

hind it lack one important factor present in the above examples: that the cultivated tree is feeble and can no longer bear fruit, since the wild branches, on being grafted, at once partake of the fat root of the tree (11:17). Admittedly both the reports from recent times and the directions given in the ancient agricultural works cited above can give us no satisfactory explanation. The former are too few and too random to carry any weight, and the latter are too obscure, as—I think—are all horticultural handbooks! Only someone with professional training could read these directions for beginners with any benefit. A further problem, which is touched upon in the literature cited, but which I will not venture to deal with, is the question of whether the wild olive tree and the oleaster are two different species or identical.

**11:18-24.** The Gentile Christian—privileged according to verse 17 in that, while the natural branches were broken off the true olive tree,[201] he was grafted in as a wild branch—is not to boast[202] against the natural branches, whether broken off or upon the tree (*Weiss*). For it is not owing to any merit of his, but through a manifestation of God's goodness, that the gospel has come to him. Only by living in God's goodness, receiving it by faith, and refraining from boasting is it possible to be part of the olive tree of the true Israel. Otherwise the Gentile Christians will suffer the same fate as did the Jews: they will fall, and thus become acquainted with God's severity.[203]

---

[201] *Lagrange* assumes of v. 19 that Paul's remark here is based upon an observation of agriculture: the other branches must be sacrificed in order that the scion may take and grow. This could agree with the thought of v. 11, but since natural branches are still left on the tree it is probably the reality contained in the metaphor rather than a possible knowledge of olive growing that has determined the statement in v. 19. It must again be stressed that God's chosen olive tree has sap enough for all the branches God intends to graft upon it.

[202] *Michel*, pp. 246-47, holds—wrongly, to my mind—that those who boast are pneumatics.

[203] As earlier (in the case of the Old Testament quotations in 9:25 f.) *Michel* holds that Paul bases 11:17-24 on an earlier tradition. The basis for this is that "his explanations are so positively defined and thought through." Against this it must be pointed out that it is wrong to assume—without giving convincing grounds for the assumption—that Paul is dependent on predecessors. It seems unfortunate that liberal exegesis, which often regarded Paul's letters as the spontaneous outcome of his emotional life, should have been

It is here evident, as *Althaus* and *Maier* rightly point out, that Paul holds no metaphysical doctrine of predestination. Just as the call is not irrevocable, neither is the obduracy. As is made clear by *Nygren*, Paul knows that the same temptation as made Israel fall also lies in wait for the Christian, and is a serious danger to him. The Jew says: "I belong to the people of inheritance." He then relies on circumcision and the promises made to his fathers, and in his self-sufficiency refuses to believe. In exactly the same way the Christian is tempted to trust in his own faith, his own Christianity. But Paul dwells only briefly on the possibility that the Gentile Christian might not continue in God's goodness; it is merely mentioned to give weight to his admonition. He then turns to what is his main interest in chapters 9-11: God's will to save. He therefore looks ahead to God's intention, which is to be realized in the future: that the broken branches will again be grafted into the olive tree. If the Gentile Christians, who are wild branches,[204] could be assimilated, how much easier will it be to restore the natural branches to the trunk from which they were broken? As *Jülicher* points out, Paul himself, who had been an unbeliever, had come to the faith through God's grace, when a heavenly vision turned this former persecutor of Christ into his servant.

**11:25.** What has hitherto been hinted at as a possibility is here propounded emphatically as a mystery, μυστήριον. Paul several times uses the word μυστήριον concerning God's plan of salvation: thus here and in I Corinthians 15:51; cf. Ephesians 1:9 (especially concerning God's plan of salvation for the Gen-

---

replaced by a general endeavor to find sources and traditions behind his remarks. Since I Cor. 13 has once more been accepted as being written by Paul, many other sources that have been analyzed might with equal justice be once again attributed to the apostle. When Paul is assumed to have taken over a tradition—as long as it is not a question of the churches in Damascus and Jerusalem—we are confronted with the same difficulty as with Cain's wife in the Old Testament: What is the origin?

[204] For παρὰ φύσιν cf. Philostratus, *Vita Apollonii*, I, 22, τὰ γὰρ παρὰ φύσιν οὔτ' ἂν γένοιτο, ταχεῖάν τε ἴσχει διαφθοράν, κἂν γένηται.

tiles); Romans 16:25 (not by Paul); Colossians 1:26 f.; possibly I Corinthians 2:1; cf. Ephesians 3:3 ff.; 3:9; 6:19.[205]

The chief content of the mystery must be that the partial hardening of Israel is limited—not merely in extent but also in time—so that it will last only until τὸ πλήρωμα τῶν ἐθνῶν εἰσέλθῃ, and then all Israel, both those who already belong to the true Israel of God (the church) and those presently hardened, will be saved (verse 26). The closing words of verse 25 are difficult. εἰσέλθῃ is generally taken to mean entering the sacred community of salvation (*Weiss*), entering the kingdom of God (*Maier*). *Sanday and Headlam* write of εἰσέλθῃ that it was used almost technically of entering the kingdom of God (or "the divine glory of life") and point to Matthew 7:21; 18:8; Mark 9:43-47. By this means, εἰσέρχεσθαι came to be used as an "absolute" construction in this same sense (Matthew 7:13; 23:13; Luke 13:24). This is true, but it is worth remarking that the most extensive usage of this term is to be found in Matthew and Mark, to a small extent in Luke, once in John (3:5) and in Acts (14:20), not at all in Paul (if not here),[206] and a number of times of εἰσέρχεσθαι εἰς τὴν κατάπαυσίν μου in Hebrews 3:11—4:11. The usage is therefore not so common that Paul can as a matter of course be regarded as using εἰσέρχεσθαι in the absolute sense here, with an implicit εἰς τὴν βασιλείαν τοῦ θεοῦ.

It is better to regard εἰσέρχεσθαι here as having the weakened meaning of "come, begin,"[207] and translate: "until the fullness of the Gentiles begins." One could question whether it is proper to make the subject of εἰσέρχεσθαι, i.e., τὸ

205 Cf. *Moe*, pp. 461-62.

206 If Paul employs this usage here, it forms a striking contrast to Matt. 8:11 f., as pointed out by Windisch in "Die Sprüche vom Eingehen in das Reich Gottes," *Zeitschrift für die Neutestamentliche Wissenschaft*, 27 (1928), p. 171.

207 Cf. *Bauer-Arndt-Gingrich*, pp. 231-32; H. G. Liddell and R. Scott, *A Greek-English Lexicon*, revised by H. S. Jones (Oxford: Clarendon, 1925) I, 494-95.

πλήρωμα τῶν ἐθνῶν, denote "the full number of the Gentiles," as do *Sanday and Headlam,* and *Maier. Sanday and Headlam* hold that τὸ πλήρωμα here denotes the totality of the Gentile world, as τὸ πλήρωμα in verse 12 denotes the totality of the Jewish people, and point to the "Jewish basis to these speculations on the complete number" in texts such as the Syriac Apocalypse of Baruch 23:5: "Before therefore the number aforesaid is fulfilled, the creature will not live again [for My spirit is the creator of life], and Sheol will receive the dead,"[208] and II Esdras 2:40-41: "Take again your full number, O Zion, and conclude the list of your people who are clothed in white, who have fulfilled the law of the Lord. The number of your children, whom you desired is full; beseech the Lord's power that your people, who have been called from the beginning, may be made holy."[209] But the number (*numerus*) in question in both texts is in Greek not πλήρωμα, but ἀριθμός. In Revelation we hear of the number of the sealed in 7:4,[210] but nowhere

[208] Charles, *op. cit.,* II, 495.

[209] Bruce Metzger, ed., *The Apocrypha of the Old Testament,* Revised Standard Version (New York: Oxford University Press, 1965). The Vulgate, of course, refers to this as IV Esdras.

[210] This is generally regarded as a symbolic number, and interpreted as referring sometimes to the Jews and sometimes to the Christians. In Rev. 6:11 the martyrs are to wait ἕως πληρωθῶσιν καὶ οἱ σύνδουλοι αὐτῶν καὶ οἱ ἀδελφοὶ αὐτῶν οἱ μέλλοντες ἀποκτέννεσθαι ὡς καὶ αὐτοί. The meaning generally attributed to this is that the number of the martyrs must first be filled (there is agreement on this in all commentaries available to me). It seems to me that this common reading is improbable. I hold by the rule laid down by Delling in *Kittel (G),* VI, 295, that πληρόω "can be restricted to a purely temporal meaning only in statements that deal specifically with the measurement of time," which must of course also be applied when "to fill up a certain measure," or "to fulfill the number of martyrs fixed by God" is the subject dealt with, the rule being that the measure or number must be indicated. It will therefore be more natural to assume here that the martyrs are to have filled up something which is lacking before God intervenes, possibly in that they are completely rested. Another possibility would be that πληρόω here means: "to satisfy (by means of a payment), to pay in full" (Friedrich Preisigke, *Wörterbuch der griechischen Papyrusurkunden,* [Berlin, 1914-27], II, col. 321; J. H. Moulton and G. Milligan, *The Vocabulary of the Greek Testament* [London: Hodder & Stoughton, 1914-29] p. 520); if so, the sentence must mean, "until they and their fellow-slaves and their brothers, who are to be slain like them, have their

in the New Testament do we hear of a number that must be termed a *numerus clausus*. There are, therefore, no grounds at all for attributing this sense to the present text, which reads τὸ πλήρωμα τῶν ἐθνῶν. Above, on 11:12, τὸ πλήρωμα αὐτῶν has been interpreted similarly to τὸ πλήρωμα τῶν ἐθνῶν here, as referring to the salvation of the group in question, with no thought of any specific number to be attained.

If this latter expression is compared with the use of πληρόω (πληροφορέω) in Romans 15:19 (πεπληρωκέναι τὸ εὐαγγέλιον τοῦ Χριστοῦ, cf. 15:15-16; Colossians 1:25: πληρῶσαι τὸν λόγον τοῦ θεοῦ, cf. verses 26 ff.; and II Timothy 4:17: ἵνα δι᾽ ἐμοῦ τὸ κήρυγμα πληροφορηθῇ καὶ ἀκούσωσιν πάντα τὰ ἔθνη)[211] we find πληρόω (πληροφορέω) used in three contexts for the full dissemination of the gospel to the Gentiles (see Romans 15:15-16; Colossians 1:26 ff.); τὸ πλήρωμα τῶν ἐθνῶν may therefore be used in a corresponding special sense. "The fullness of the Gentiles" then signifies the achievement of the goal toward which Paul is striving during his preaching of the gospel to the Gentiles: the completion of that preaching. When this has been concluded, the end can come (Matthew 24:14), Antichrist will be revealed in the temple at Jerusalem (II Thessalonians 2:3-4), and soon Christ will come to judge and to save.[212]

"The fullness of the Gentiles," therefore, is not, as we have tried to show, a specific number to be attained, i.e., a full number. This would introduce a notion of predestination which, as has been demonstrated, is alien to Paul's way of thinking in

reward." This reward or satisfaction can, it seems in the context, only mean that God exercises judgment and vengeance on the persecutors (cf. II Thess. 1:5 f.; I Thess. 2:16; Matt. 23:34-36). The prevailing interpretation, as referring to the specific number of martyrs, is based upon parallels from the late Jewish apocalyptic literature (IV Esdras 4:36 f.; Syriac Apocalypse of Baruch 30:2; cf. Volz, *op. cit.*, p. 140) which deal with the righteous. There is no parallel in late Jewish literature for the idea that the martyrs also have a specific number that must be filled before God can deliver judgment.

[211] Cf. PSM, pp. 329, 332-33.

[212] *Ibid.*, chap. 2.

Romans 9-11. There is no mention in any New Testament book of such a limiting number. "The fullness of the Gentiles" must signify the goal that the totality of the Gentile world—admittedly in a representative form—should hear the gospel, that is, both that the gospel should be preached to them, and that they should hear and believe.[213] This fullness, which according to Matthew 24:14 leads to the last phase of the eschatological events surrounding the revelation of Antichrist, is here regarded as the impetus to the salvation of the Jews. Since Paul, according to II Thessalonians 2:6-7, also believes that the conversion of the Gentiles will lead to the coming of Antichrist, it is a natural supposition that the conversion of the Jews is supposed to take place in the age of Antichrist, or at the conclusion of that period.[214]

Unfortunately we know very little about Paul's eschatological ideas. If he shared the conceptions found in the Synoptic Gospels, particularly in Matthew, it must be assumed that—since in this matter he goes beyond them—he imagined the conversion of all Israel as occurring at the time of Antichrist, or immediately before the Second Coming.[215] In the latter case, the conversion of Israel might be the event that will bring about the Second Coming, just as "the fullness of the Gentiles" (that the gospel be first preached to all the Gentiles) was the prerequisite for the appearance of Antichrist. The account in Matthew 24 is at all events obviously of Jewish-Christian origin, unshaped by Gentile Christians. The Christians whose troubles are under discussion are Jewish Christians, and the Gentiles are mentioned only in the verse that foretells that the gospel will be preached to them (Matthew 24:14; Mark 13:10; this passage is characteristically lacking in Luke).

[213] *Lietzmann* paraphrases τὸ πλήρωμα αὐτῶν (the Jews') in v. 12 as "die völlige Bekehrung Israels."

[214] Test. Dan 6:4, Οἶδε [ὁ ἐχθρὸς] γὰρ ὅτι ἐν ᾗ ἡμέρᾳ ἐπιστρέψει 'Ισραήλ, συντελεσθήσεται ἡ βασιλεία τοῦ ἐχθροῦ.

[215] On the latter possibility see *Schlatter's* interpretation of "life from the dead" in 11:15 (p. 127 above).

The question now is whether Luke, which seems to presuppose the destruction of Jerusalem, is influenced by Paul's way of thinking when its description of the fall of Jerusalem ends with: καὶ Ἰερουσαλὴμ ἔσται πατουμένη ὑπὸ ἐθνῶν, ἄχρι, οὗ πληρωθῶσιν καιροὶ ἐθνῶν (Luke 21:24). The expressions are of course not identical with those in Paul, and cannot have quite the same significance. The question is, however, whether these expressions do not nevertheless denote a modification of the earlier Synoptic view of the future, a modification which is either along the lines followed by Paul, or shows that Luke reveals Palestinian Jewish Christian presuppositions on this point when he maintains that the fate of Jerusalem, and thus Israel's fortunes, will be changed when the times of the Gentiles are at an end—not in the sense that the Gentiles will no longer rule over the Jews, but in the sense that the Gentiles will receive the gospel. At the time of this eschatologically important event the destiny of the Jews will be changed, in that the destiny of the holy city is symptomatic of God's attitude to the people, and the sufferings of the latter are all God's punishment.

**11:26-27.** After the fullness of the Gentiles has come, and as a consequence of it, all Israel—i.e., the Jews living in the last days, which to Paul means the present—will be saved. *Sanday and Headlam* interpret πᾶς Ἰσραήλ as "Israel as a whole, Israel as a nation, and not as necessarily including every individual Israelite." This is correct. "All Israel" denotes "the remnant" together with "the rest" (cf. 11:5-7), and although it stands in contrast to "the remnant," there is no question of completeness. All the categories of *Heilsgeschichte*—the Gentiles and Israel, the "remnant," and the church—are saved or rejected in their entirety, but the salvation of the individual cannot be assumed from God's election and salvation of the particular totality to which he belongs. The fate of the individual is determined by Christ at the Judgment.

In the text quoted by Paul, the first three lines (as far as διαθήκη) derive from Isaiah 59:20-21 (as an essential change it may be mentioned that ἔνεκεν Σιὼν has become ἐκ Σιὼν), while the fourth line is a free rendering of Isaiah 27:9. These various expressions may be regarded merely as proof that all Israel will be saved. But there is the possibility that the text is intended to give an eschatological picture of Christ: Christ descends from heaven, and from (Paul has ἐκ) Mount Zion appears to Israel. This feature can be directly combined with another concrete feature concerning Christ at his reappearance (II Thessalonians 2:4, 8), that at his Second Coming he will at once destroy Antichrist, who has taken his seat in God's temple in Jerusalem.

Nothing is said directly of the results brought about by Antichrist in Jerusalem and Palestine, but Antichrist is possibly connected with the apostasy (II Thessalonians 2:3),[216] and his lying miracles and unrighteous deceptions (verses 9-10) influence a large number (possibly a majority; cf. Matthew 24:10-12) of people, who perish.[217] In all, we get the following picture of the Second Coming: Christ descends in Jerusalem,[218] destroys Antichrist on Zion,[219] and from thence appears to Israel to save it.[220] And then all Israel will be saved.[221] If Matthew 23:39, "For I tell you, you will not see me again, until you say, 'Blessed be he who comes in the name of the Lord,' " is interpreted as referring to a final conversion of the Jews after the destruction of Jerusalem, it is a parallel to this

[216] If the apostasy and the Antichrist are not here, as in the Synoptic Apocalypse in Matthew, two different parts of the eschatological drama (cf. my *Petrus und Paulus in der Offenbarung Johannis* [Copenhagen, 1950] pp. 52-55).

[217] A later period assumed that the Jews would follow the Antichrist for a time at least; cf. W. Bousset, *Der Antichrist* (Göttingen, 1895) pp. 108 ff; cf. pp. 104 ff.

[218] Rom. 11:26; II Thess. 2:4, 8; Acts 1:4 (cf. PSM, pp. 210-12).

[219] II Thess. 2:8; cf. Rom. 11:26.

[220] Rom. 11:26-27.

[221] Rom. 11:26; cf. Acts 3:19-26; 5:30-31.

passage. But the interpretation of Matthew 23:39 is uncertain, and there is no reference in Matthew 24 to the conversion of Israel in the last days.

## 11:28-32. Behind the casting-off of Israel is God's intention of consigning all to disobedience that he may have mercy upon all.

**11:28.** It has been questioned whether ἐχθροί is to be understood in the active sense, as "hostile," or in the passive, as "hated." It is difficult to reach a definite conclusion. The parallelism with the following sentence seems to indicate that the two adjectives ἐχθροί and ἀγαπητοί are to be read in the same sense, viz., as the passive, and it has earlier been stated that the one not chosen is hated by God, namely in the Malachi quotation in 9:13, "Esau I hated." On the other hand, ἐχθρός is always used in the active sense elsewhere in the New Testament, and the context favors this reading. Israel is here seen as the persecutor of the Gentile churches, the hardened and contrary people, nevertheless beloved for the sake of the patriarchs, whom God elected. Here again one might ask, with *Jülicher* earlier, why God here takes account of ancestry when Paul in chapter 9 so strongly denied that one's descent is of any importance for salvation. But Paul did not deny the importance of ancestry, but only man's right to use it in making claims upon God. But now God, of his free mercy and for the sake of the patriarchs and his earlier promises, does not forget his people Israel.

**11:29.** Israel is beloved of God for the patriarchs' sake, because God does not take back from his people the gifts of grace listed in 9:4 f., especially their call to salvation. Since chapter 10 gave an account of God's calling of his people in the days of Jesus and the apostles, the calling mentioned here may either be identical with—or at all events include—Israel's call in early times. *Pallis* has pointed out that ἀμεταμέλητα means "irrevocable," and is a legal term. "This statement," he says, "probably reflects the Jewish idea, with which our author as a Jew was doubtless impregnated, that God is bound legally, as it were, to carry out his covenant." While there can be no doubt that the first point is correct,[222] it seems misleading to assume that in Romans the author would say that God is, so to speak, legally bound to carry out his covenant. And yet in Galatians 3 Paul has in fact used the legal rules of the day to prove that God's promises remain valid. In Galatians 3:15, "no one annuls even a man's will,[223] or adds to it, once it has been ratified," and in verse 17, "the law, which came four hundred and thirty years afterward, does not annul a covenant previously ratified by God, so as to make the promise void." These passages in Galatians are, however, introduced by the formula, "to give a human example, brethren." It is, therefore, correct with *Bauer-Arndt-Gingerich* to assume here the meaning of "irrevocable," but to dismiss any implication that God is legally bound.

**11:30-31.** Paul shows how obvious God's intention is to save all Israel. Once the Gentiles were disobedient, but now they have obtained mercy through the disobedience of the Jews. In the same way, the Jews are now disobedient in order that they may in turn obtain mercy, the same mercy as was shown to the Gentiles.[224] It may seem surprising that the former conduct of

222 ἀμεταμέλητος, see *Pallis, ad. loc.;* Fr. Preisigke, *op. cit.,* I, and the same work (ed. E. Kiessling), 1944, IV, 1; *Bauer-Arndt-Gingrich;* and ἀμετανόητος in Moulton and Milligan, *op. cit.* In *Zeitschrift für die Neutestamentliche Wissenschaft,* 18 (1917), p. 91, note 1, Eger assumes that ἀμεταμέλητον must be a legal term.

223 διαθήκη occurs in Rom. 11:27 in the quotation from Isa. 59:20-21. Nestle and, e.g., Johannes Behm, *Der Begriff διαθήκη im Neuen Testament* (Leipzig: A. Deichertsche Verlagsbuchhandlung, 1912), pp. 43-44, hold that Jer. 31 (LXX, 38):33 f. is also to be heard in the compound quotation, Rom. 11:26-27.

224 In "Vier Worte des Römerbriefs," *Symbolae Biblicae Upsalienses,* 3 (1944), pp. 14-17, M. Dibelius has suggested, following Blass-Debrunner (trans. Funk), *op. cit.,* sec. 196, p. 105, that the two datives ἀπειθείᾳ and ἐλέει (Dibelius terms them a kind of *dativus commodi*) should be interpreted

the Gentiles should be described as disobedience. This was not the case in Romans 1:18 ff., even though it is possible to label as disobedience the negative attitude of the Gentiles toward the revelation of God in creation. In Ephesians 2:2 we find the Gentiles described as οἱ υἱοὶ τῆς ἀπειθείας, while the same expression is used in Ephesians 5:6 and Colossians 3:6 (introduced from Ephesians 5:6) in a more general, moral sense. Elsewhere the verb ἀπειθέω is used of the Jews. Romans 2:8; 10:21 (quotation); 15:31. In Hebrews the substantive and the verb are used concerning the Israelites' disobedience, 3:18; 4:6, 11. In Hebrews 11:31 the verb is used concerning the disobedience of the inhabitants of Jericho, and in I Peter 3:20 concerning the disobedience of the Flood generation, while in the remaining instances in I Peter (2:8; 3:1; 4:17) it is used in a moral sense without distinction between Jews and Gentiles. It is therefore correct to say that the expression "disobedience" has been chosen with the object of drawing a close parallel between the conduct of the Gentiles and that of the Jews, in order that the salvation of the latter may also appear as a close parallel to the salvation of the Gentiles, which is already a fact.

It seems best to include τῷ ὑμετέρῳ ἐλέει in the succeeding clause of intention, so that it denotes the *dativus instrumentalis*, and forms a parallel to τῇ τούτων ἀπειθείᾳ (*Weiss*), and not with *Kühl, Lagrange,* and *Lietzmann* to connect it with ἠπείθησαν. One notes that the disobedience of the Gentiles belongs to the past, while their salvation, together with the disobedience of the Jews and their salvation, (νυν appears three times) takes place in the present.

**11:32.** This sums up what has been said in the immediately preceding comparison between the Gentiles and Jews, and in

in a way that permits the following paraphrase (p. 17): "For as you in the old days were disobedient to God but have now come to experience grace while these others are becoming disobedient, so these have also become disobedient while you are experiencing grace, in order that they may someday find grace as well."

the whole of the preceding passage, chapters 9-11: God has consigned all to disobedience, that he may have mercy upon all. This is the way to salvation opened by God to all, in which, regardless of the disobedience of all, he offers them salvation through the apostles of Jesus, if they will only believe and confess Jesus Christ. Thus the same way to salvation is open to all, Jews and Gentiles alike.

There are two possible interpretations of this final verse, first that it means all Jews, and secondly that it means all men, both Jews and Gentiles. The first possibility, which is maintained by *Zahn*, accords with the emphasis of the passage immediately preceding (11:28-31), and indeed of the whole section (chapters 9-11) namely, the Jews and their destiny. Here in 11:32 οἱ πάντες would be a plural rendering of the πᾶς Ἰσραήλ of 11:26, forming the conclusion of an account that began with the οὐ πάντες of 9:6, and can now end with οἱ πάντες.

If the other possibility is accepted—that 11:32 is speaking of both Jews and Gentiles here, at the end of a section concerned with the Jews—then the point is that the way of salvation elected by God for all men is the one common to Gentiles and Jews. This is a way which the latter are now beginning to follow, though they have only reached the state of disobedience, and as disobedient men have yet to receive God's mercy. The difference between the two possibilities is only slight.

## 11:33-36. Praise of God for his salvation of Gentiles and Jews.

The section comprising chapters 9-11 ends with a doxology. The magnificent description of God's love in Christ at the end of chapter 8 has been followed with curious abruptness by the painful consideration of Israel's obduracy. Now, having been able to point to a light in the darkness surrounding the fate of Israel, and to show God's mercy toward Israel's obduracy and his all-merciful grace in the salvation of all Israel at this time, Paul turns with his readers to that praise of God which to him is the goal of his mental endeavor to trace God's working in the world. In I Corinthians 2:12 he said of the maturer Christians: "Now we have received not the spirit of the world, but the Spirit which is from God, that we might understand the gifts bestowed on us by God."

Paul praises the riches and wisdom and knowledge of God, which are boundless. His judgments and his ways, which show his wisdom and knowledge, are unsearchable by men. These are inscrutable, and no man can be God's counselor. And God's riches are so boundless that it is always he who gives.[225] No one can give him anything because all things are already his. Verse 34 quotes Isaiah 40:13 (with the addition of $\gamma \acute{a} \rho$), a passage also quoted in I Corinthians 2:16 in a slightly different form. In verse 35 Paul goes on to quote Job 41:11 (Heb. 41:3; Vulg. 41:2), not according to the LXX, but presumably from another Greek translation apparently used by him in the case of Job.[226]

*Sanday and Headlam,* and *Billerbeck* III, pp. 294-5, quote many late Jewish parallels to verse 36, while *Kühl,* and particularly *Lietzmann,* refer to and quote Hellenistic material in connection with the triadic formula.[227] *Althaus* rightly dis-

[225] Günther Bornkamm, "Der Lobpreis Gottes (Rom. 11:33-36)," (*Das Ende des Gesetzes, op. cit.,* pp. 70-75), conjectures that the three questions in 11:34-35 are attached in reverse order to the three concepts, $\pi \lambda o \hat{v} \tau o s$, $\sigma o \phi \acute{\iota} a$, $\gamma v \hat{\omega} \sigma \iota s$ in v. 33. Owing to the difficulty of distinguishing clearly between $\sigma o \phi \acute{\iota} a$ and $\gamma v \hat{\omega} \sigma \iota s$ in the two questions in v. 34, I prefer the interpretation given in the present text.

[226] See the excursus by H. Lietzmann in his *An die Galater* ("Handbuch zum Neuen Testament," Vol. 10), Tübingen: J. C. B. Mohr, 1933, p. 34. For the possible use of further texts from Job in Rom. 11:33-35, see R. P. C. Hanson, "St. Paul's Quotations of the Book of Job," *Theology,* 53 (1950) p. 251 ff.

[227] See also now the material in *Michel,* and H. Almqvist, *op. cit.,* pp. 88-9. For the Hellenistic material in particular see Eduard Norden, *Agnostos Theos* (Leipzig, 1913) pp. 240-50 and 347-54. L. G. Champion, *op. cit.,* pp. 126-28, compares Rom. 11:33-36 with I Thess. 5:23 because both passages contain formulae deriving from the LXX, Judaism, and Hellenism.

misses the suggestion that this similarity in wording between the Hellenistic material and Paul's formula has anything to do with a common source of ideas. Paul's formula finds its explanation in Romans 9-11, where he speaks of a personal God who has made known his saving will.

# Indexes

# I. Index of Source Citations

## 1. OLD TESTAMENT

147

## 2. APOCRYPHAL AND OTHER LATE JEWISH LITERATURE

## 3. PHILO

## 4. NEW TESTAMENT

## 5. ANCIENT AND EARLY CHURCH WRITERS

## II. Index of Authors

*Type,* 11 on 13 and 10 on 11 Garamond; 11 on 13 Porson Greek
*Display,* Tempo, Metrolite, Caledonia, and Garamond
*Paper,* 'R' Antique